American Louvre

D1268465

Smithsonian American Art Museum, Washington, DC,
in association with D Giles Limited, London

American Louvre

A History of the Renwick Gallery Building

Charles J. Robertson

Furthermore:
a program of the J. M. Kaplan Fund

The Museum is grateful to Furthermore,
a program of the J. M. Kaplan Fund,
for its support of this publication.

Contents

Foreword   7

Mr. Corcoran   9

Renwick and Corcoran   15

Design of the New Gallery   25

The War Begins   33

General Meigs   39

Reclaiming the Gallery   47

Opening the Gallery   51

The Later Years   61

The Court of Claims   73

Saving the Building   81

Restoring the Building   85

The Renwick Today   91

Notes   100

Selected Bibliography   102

Illustration Sources and Credits   104

Index   106

Foreword

*T*he reopening of the Renwick Gallery after two years of comprehensive renovation is a grand occasion to recall this landmark building's noble history and future promise. The building began life as the Corcoran Gallery of Art, designed in 1858 as the first purpose-built art museum in America and the first art museum in the nation's capital. The gallery later moved to new quarters, and the building then served as the US Court of Claims for more than 60 years. Since 1972, the building has been known as the Renwick Gallery, devoted to crafts and decorative arts as a branch of the Smithsonian American Art Museum.

Charles J. Robertson, a scholar in decorative arts and historical architecture, tells the colorful story of the building's initial glory, decline, and rebirth over a period of 160 years. He reveals how a new pavilion of the Louvre inspired William Wilson Corcoran and James Renwick to create a highly ornamented building in the center of federal Washington that would encourage "American genius" and demonstrate that American art could rival that of Europe. His book complements his earlier work, *Temple of Invention: History of a National Landmark,* which tells the story of the Patent Office Building, home of the Smithsonian American Art Museum.

Today, strengthened for the next half century, the Renwick Gallery embarks on a new chapter of its illustrious life as a champion of art in the nation's capital and a welcoming site of discovery for all.

Elizabeth Broun
The Margaret and Terry Stent Director
Smithsonian American Art Museum

1   **View of Georgetown, DC.**
William Corcoran was born and spent his early
years in this small but thriving community on
the banks of the Potomac River.

Mr. Corcoran

The words "Dedicated to Art" are chiseled in stone on its facade. It is the first building in the United States constructed exclusively as a public art museum. Its design is modeled on the Louvre in Paris, and it was once called the "American Louvre." It helped launch a new style of architecture in this country. It was created by two remarkable men, William Corcoran and James Renwick.

William Wilson Corcoran was born December 2, 1798, in Georgetown in the District of Columbia. At that time, Georgetown was a small but prosperous port city on the Potomac River that still had its own separate form of local government. William's father, Thomas, in 1783 at age 29 had emigrated from Limerick, Ireland, to Baltimore, where he worked as a clerk in his uncle's shipping business. Thomas married Hannah Lemmon of Baltimore and in 1788 settled in Georgetown, where he established a leather and tanning business. Thomas prospered, invested in real estate, and held positions as magistrate, postmaster, and mayor of Georgetown (fig. 1).

The marriage produced six children, of which William was the second youngest. William attended private schools and enrolled in Georgetown College for one year. But he was impatient to dive into the world of commerce, so at age 17, against the objection of his father, he joined his two older brothers, Thomas and James, in their dry goods business. With his brothers' assistance, William then opened his own dry goods store in Georgetown, later expanding it as a wholesale auction and commission business. Unfortunately, the panic of 1823 precipitated the demise of his business, and with debts of $28,000 he was, to his chagrin, forced to declare bankruptcy. After briefly managing his father's real estate interests, Corcoran secured a clerkship in Washington's oldest bank and later a position in the Bank of the United States as manager of its real estate and debt holdings.

Corcoran had a reputation as a ladies' man, but at age 36 he fell in love with 16-year-old Louise Amory Morris, the daughter of naval commodore Charles Morris, who had distinguished himself in the War of 1812. Louise's parents were adamantly opposed to her marriage to this Irish upstart, who had once failed in business and was 20 years her senior. It was a rocky courtship, with Corcoran protesting to Louise about her parents' objections, "I am not the beggar they would fain to persuade you." Finally, in December 1835 the couple eloped to Baltimore. Upon their return, Corcoran wrote to the commodore, "Your daughter is now under the protection of a husband whose aim will ever be to promote her happiness." Corcoran attempted reconciliation with her parents, which was to occur only with the birth of the first child. The marriage ultimately produced three children, only one of whom, also named Louise, lived to adulthood. Sadly, Corcoran's wife died of tuberculosis only five years after the marriage. Corcoran never remarried. Decades later he would place a marble bust of the commodore in his new art museum.

By 1837, Corcoran was able to open a small brokerage office near the US Treasury Building. Several developments coalesced around this time to Corcoran's advantage. The Bank of the United States had closed in 1836, leaving its extensive accounts to be taken over by private

2 **Corcoran and Riggs Bank Building** (demolished). Corcoran purchased the building on the right in 1845 for his bank (shown here ca. 1893). The house on the left was the chief clerk's residence.

banks. Also, Corcoran was favored with the patronage of the nationally influential bankers Elisha Riggs and George Peabody. In 1840, Corcoran formed a partnership with Elisha's son, George Washington Riggs, who had returned from an apprenticeship in London with Peabody. Together they established the banking firm Corcoran and Riggs, which soon became the major financial agent and depository for government accounts. The firm by 1845 was able to purchase the former home of the Bank of the United States, across Pennsylvania Avenue from the Treasury Building (fig. 2). Two years later Corcoran paid off with interest

3 **William Wilson Corcoran.**
His fortune had been made in
banking and investments.

all of the old debts incurred in his bankruptcy 24 years earlier, even
though he had no legal obligation to do so.

The transaction that made Corcoran's fortune, however, was
his bank's underwriting of the bond issues needed to finance the
Mexican-American War of 1846–48. When $12 million of the bonds
failed to sell in the United States at their desired price, Corcoran
sailed to London and offered them on the European market. When
they rose to 119½, the firm reaped a windfall. With his fortune secured
by this and other business ventures, Corcoran in 1854 withdrew from
Corcoran and Riggs, which subsequently became Riggs and Company,
and essentially retired from active business, though he continued
to pursue and enlarge his extensive private holdings in real estate,
railroads, insurance, and utilities (fig. 3).

Renwick and Corcoran

*T*he Smithsonian Institution was officially founded by Act of Congress in 1846 to implement James Smithson's unique mandate "for the increase and diffusion of knowledge among men." Princeton physics professor Joseph Henry was appointed to head the institution with the title of Secretary. The Corcoran and Riggs bank was chosen to manage the Smithsonian's financial affairs, which resulted in William Corcoran's becoming a close friend of Joseph Henry. The first order of business for the Smithsonian was the construction of a building prominent and distinguished enough to signal the importance of its mission (fig. 4). A national architectural competition was held for the design of the building. From the 12 entries submitted, the winner was 27-year-old James Renwick Jr.

James Renwick Jr. was born November 1, 1818, at his grandmother's country home in Bloomingdale, New York, but spent his life and professional career in New York City. His mother was Margaret Brevoort Renwick, a seventh-generation descendant of the venerable and wealthy Brevoort family. His father, James Renwick Sr., was also from a prominent family engaged in transatlantic trade. James Sr. received a BA and MA from Columbia College and subsequently held a professorship there in natural philosophy. He had a keen interest in astronomy, mineralogy, and architecture, and he published papers on a variety of topics. He and his wife were well connected with the intellectual and social elite of New York City.

The second of three brothers, James Jr. was also educated at Columbia College, where he was offered courses in mathematics, physics, and mechanics, as well as the classics; architecture was not taught at Columbia until 1881. James received a bachelor's degree in engineering at age 17 in 1836 and an MA

4 **Smithsonian Institution "Castle."** James Renwick's first commission in Washington was a major coup at age 27.

5   **Grace Church.** This 1843 commission in New York City established Renwick's reputation.

6 **James Renwick.** He was Corcoran's architect for many projects. Here he holds a drawing of St. Patrick's Cathedral, his best-known building in New York City.

three years later. He first worked as a surveyor and engineer for the Erie Railroad and then on the extensive Croton Reservoir Aqueduct project that brought water to New York City. In 1851 he married Anna Lloyd Aspinwall, whose wealthy father owned a notable art collection, but they had no children.

James was only 24 when, in 1843, he was awarded the design of a new building for the affluent and fashionable congregation of Grace Episcopal Church at Broadway and Tenth Street. This was a remarkable achievement, since Renwick was essentially self-taught as an architect and since this was the first building he had ever designed and constructed. The church in the mostly French Gothic Revival style was an instant success and made his reputation. Its dramatically tall, thin spire was immediately christened "Renwick's toothpick" (fig. 5). Other commissions soon followed. Between 1843 and 1859, Renwick's office completed designs for six major churches in New York City. During this period, he won commissions for two hotels, two hospitals, a bank, and numerous private residences.

Renwick's most famous building in New York City was the massive St. Patrick's Cathedral, begun in 1858 and completed in 1879. The style is a skillful blend of French, English, and German Gothic. At the time it was surprising that a Protestant architect had been selected for the most imposing structure in the Catholic hierarchy, but Renwick had proven himself the best candidate for the job (fig. 6).

7 **Chapel at Oak Hill Cemetery.** The chapel was Corcoran's earliest commission for Renwick, in 1850.

The Smithsonian's "Castle" was Renwick's first major commission outside New York. The plan was for a grandiose and picturesque structure with multiple towers in the Norman Romanesque style. Construction began in 1848 and was completed in 1855 (see fig. 4). The building, the first important structure on the Mall, received national notice. It and its architect also attracted the notice of William Corcoran. With new wealth at

8   **Town houses** (demolished). This row of houses was designed by Renwick for Corcoran in 1852 as an investment.

9   (overleaf) **Corcoran's mansion** (demolished). This was his home on Lafayette Square until his death. Renwick added the top floor and side wings in 1850.

(See map, p. 26, for location of properties.)

his disposal, Corcoran had a number of building projects in mind, and he needed an architect to execute them. Renwick was a logical choice.

In 1848, Corcoran purchased 12½ acres of hilly terrain in Georgetown for a cemetery. Congress chartered Oak Hill Cemetery the next year, and the necessary work of grading, laying out the plots, and constructing roads and paths began. But a chapel was needed, and Corcoran hired Renwick to design it. The resulting building, an elegant gem in Ruskinian Gothic style, was constructed in 1850–53 of striated gray granite trimmed in red sandstone (fig. 7). The total cost was $9,400. (The chapel was meticulously restored, inside and out, in 2013.) Corcoran later retained architect Thomas U. Walter to design a monumental marble tempietto as a tomb for himself and his family on a hill in the cemetery. Renwick designed two additional projects for Corcoran. One, constructed in 1852–53 (since demolished), comprised six handsome four-story town houses (fig. 8) as an investment on I Street and Vermont Avenue, only two blocks from Corcoran's home. The other was Harewood, a country retreat or "lodge" for Corcoran, situated north of the city near the Old Soldiers' Home.

During this period, Corcoran embarked upon a course of influential and wide-ranging philanthropy that he would pursue for the rest of his life. He donated funds or land or both for the Georgetown public school system, the Washington Horticultural Society (of which he was president),

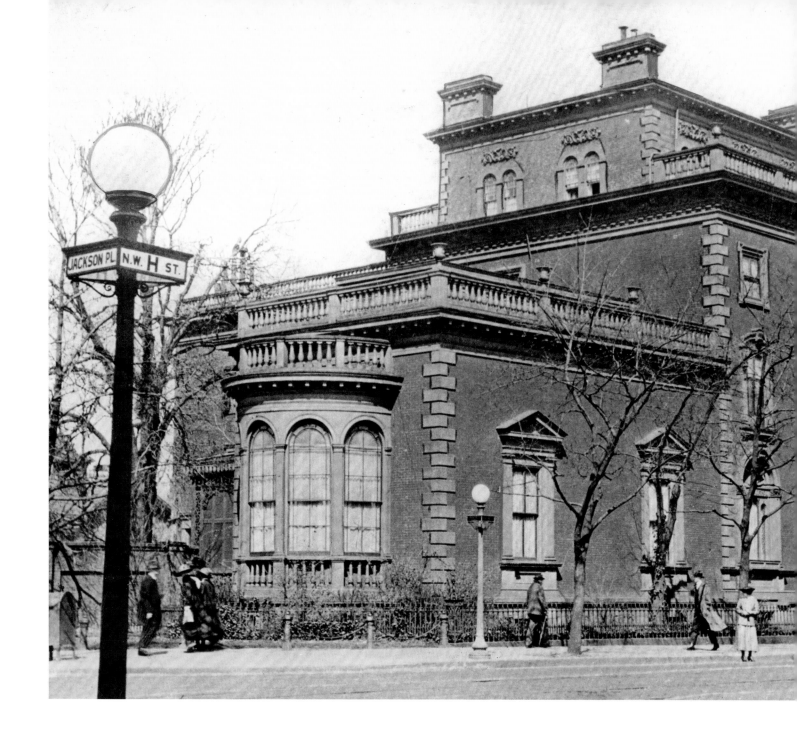

St. John's Episcopal Church, Trinity Episcopal Church, the City Orphan Asylum, the Washington Monument, and even the Irish famine.

Corcoran's affluence and influence at this stage in his life required a residence commensurate with his position in the nation's capital. In 1849 he purchased for $14,000 a three-story Federal-style house constructed in 1828 on Lafayette Square, which was immediately north of the White House and the most prestigious residential neighborhood in the city at the time (fig. 9). The house had been owned by Corcoran's friend Daniel Webster while Webster was secretary of state under presidents Harrison and Tyler. Corcoran retained James Renwick to enlarge and update the building in the then fashionable Italianate style. Renwick added a fourth floor and a large wing on each side: one wing to house a combination ballroom and gallery, and the other to house a library and a dining room, both with 28-foot-high ceilings (figs. 10, 11). Interior decoration of the house was handled by the prominent New York firm Ringuet-Leprince and L. Marcotte. The two-and-one-half acre grounds in the rear were landscaped by noted designer Andrew Jackson Downing.

It was a showplace and was Corcoran's residence for the rest of his life. He used it to maximum advantage, hosting opulent entertainments, weekly stag parties, and an annual ball for members of Congress. Washington's business and political elite sought invitations. Corcoran was active in Democratic politics and a friend of presidents Fillmore and Buchanan, among other prominent statesmen of the day. Benjamin Ogle Tayloe, Corcoran's neighbor on Lafayette Square, had this to say about Corcoran's parties: "Mr. Corcoran, by his magnificent entertainments, threw all others in the shade. . . . His splendid dinners are well remembered; the most grand, with a fete of Senators on each side of the table, intermixed with foreign and Cabinet ministers."

Around this time Corcoran began to collect art to fill his new residence and gallery. During trips abroad, he acquired contemporary European paintings in the academic taste popular in that era. As early as 1850 he began

10 **Ballroom of Corcoran's mansion.**
It also served as Corcoran's picture
gallery.

collecting works by American artists such as Thomas Cole, John Frederick
Kensett, Jasper Francis Cropsey, and George Inness. His most celebrated
acquisition, however, was his purchase in 1851 of Hiram Powers's *Greek Slave*
for $5,000. This was the first of five replicas of the original sculpture autho-
rized by Powers and carved in his studio in Florence. Corcoran installed it in
pride of place in the bay window of the gallery in his home.

By 1855 he was opening the gallery to the public on two days each week.
Two years later he published the first catalogue of his art collection. Of the 83
listed works, 34 were by American artists, underscoring Corcoran's belief that
American artists could do as well artistically as their European counterparts.

11   Library of Corcoran's mansion.
A small statue of George Washington,
one of Corcoran's heroes, is on the
bookcase at far right.

Design of the New Gallery

*W*illiam Corcoran took an extensive tour of Europe in 1855, armed with a letter of introduction from Joseph Henry on behalf of the Smithsonian's Board of Regents, and was impressed by the architecture of Paris. Corcoran visited the Exposition Universelle and saw the new wing of the Louvre, then nearing completion. When Napoleon III became emperor of France in 1852, he initiated a massive building campaign that transformed Paris into the city we know today, with wide boulevards, public parks, and iconic buildings. His reign (1852–70) became known as the Second Empire to distinguish it from the first empire of his uncle, Napoleon Bonaparte. For the venerable Louvre, Napoleon III retained architect Louis Visconti to "complete" the structure by adding a huge north wing connecting it to the Tuileries Palace. The new style respected earlier parts of the Louvre in general massing, but signaled a difference in architectural treatment (fig. 12).

James Renwick had also traveled to Europe in 1854–55, with the New York Board of Charities and Corrections; he, too, was deeply impressed with the Louvre's new wing. Upon returning to Washington, Corcoran increasingly realized that he needed more space for his burgeoning collection and began to think about a building or gallery to showcase it for public visitation. He had been involved with art organizations in the city and saw the need to bring an appreciation of art to a wider audience. He purchased five lots two blocks from his home at a prominent location: the corner of 17th Street and Pennsylvania Avenue, directly across from the War Department Building (replaced later by the State, War, and Navy Building) and within view of the White House (fig. 13). He gave Renwick the task of designing his new gallery. They decided that its style would

12 **Napoleon III wing of the Louvre.** This new wing (1852-57) was Renwick's inspiration for the Corcoran Gallery's design, but on a much smaller scale.

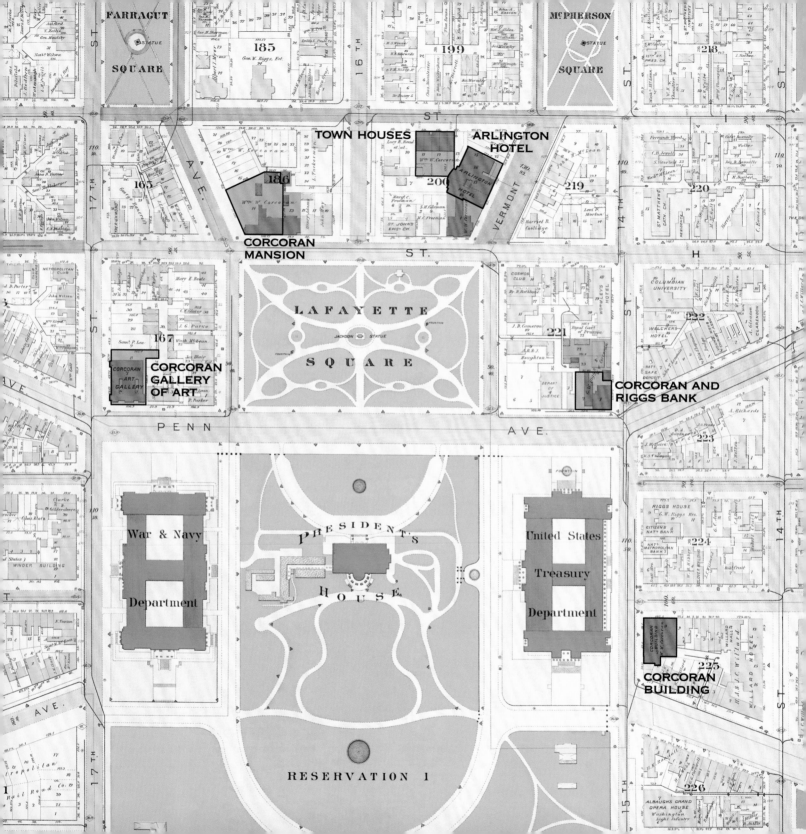

FARRAGUT SQUARE

McPHERSON SQUARE

185

199

213

TOWN HOUSES

ARLINGTON HOTEL

165

186

200

219

220

CORCORAN MANSION

L A F A Y E T T E

167

JACKSON STATUE

221

222

S Q U A R E

CORCORAN GALLERY OF ART

CORCORAN AND RIGGS BANK

223

P E N N   A V E.

War & Navy

Department

P R E S I D E N T ' S

H O U S E

United States

Treasury

Department

RIGGS HOUSE

224

225

CORCORAN BUILDING

R E S E R V A T I O N   1

226

THE NEW GALLERY OF ART, WASHINGTON, D. C.
RENWICK & AUCHMUTY, ARCHITECTS.

13 **Buildings once owned by Corcoran** are shown in red on this 1887 map. Except for the Corcoran Gallery, all of these buildings were later demolished.

14 **Renwick's design for the gallery.** This drawing was published in 1859 in the influential *Architects and Mechanics Journal*.

be based generally on the new wing of the Louvre but necessarily on a much smaller scale to fit the site and at half the height of the Louvre. Renwick readily acknowledged his debt to the Louvre but noted that "the details and proportions are entirely different." It is Renwick's creative handling of architectural elements that enhances the originality of the building's design.

In 1858, Renwick drew up plans and 16 pages of specifications for the gallery that were approved by Corcoran (fig. 14). The design featured

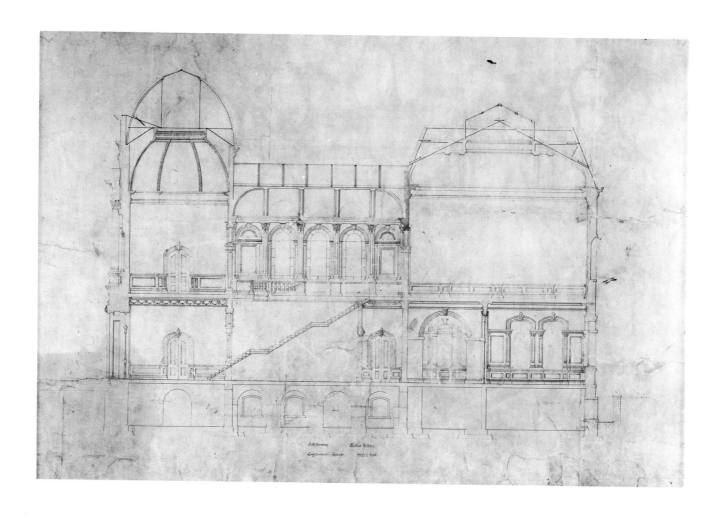

15 Cross section of the gallery.
On the second floor, the Grand Salon is on the right and the Octagon Room on the left.

a central pavilion topped by a domed mansard roof. The smaller end pavilions were capped by truncated pyramidal mansard roofs. The tops of the pavilions sported ornamental cresting made of zinc. Niches on the second story were intended for figural sculptures. The side corners of the pavilions on the first floor were emphasized by vermiculated quoins (decorative cornerstones) that supported columns and pilasters on the second story. Renwick added a whimsical American touch by incorporating corncobs among the acanthus leaves of the columns' capitals (see fig. 40), inspired by Benjamin Latrobe's earlier use of corn in his capitals at the US Capitol.

Renwick chose a contrasting palette of materials for the building: for the facades, Baltimore pressed red brick richly ornamented with architectural elements of brown Bellville sandstone from New Jersey, and purple Welsh slate for the roofs. The interior included a grand flight of stairs to the second floor, which featured a main picture gallery (the Grand Salon) and an octagonal room that was specifically designed for *The Greek Slave* (fig. 15). Renwick's elevation for the gallery's facade was published in 1859 in the influential *Architects and Mechanics Journal* (see fig. 14). Construction began that year and proceeded rapidly.

The building embodies two concepts that seem unremarkable today but were revolutionary at the time: the creation of a museum designed exclusively for art, and the introduction of a new style of architecture to the United States. Earlier public buildings exhibited art, such as the Wadsworth Atheneum in Hartford, Connecticut, which functioned as a library, among other purposes, but up to this time none had been devoted entirely to the display of art. Corcoran made clear the purpose of his building by placing on the facade, in prominent raised stone letters, "Dedicated to Art." Interestingly enough, Corcoran's name did not appear on the outside of the building. Also remarkable was the gallery's inauguration in Washington, which, with a population of about 60,000 in 1858, was considered a cultural backwater. The streets, except for Pennsylvania Avenue, were unpaved, and there was no sewer system.

The Corcoran Gallery is largely credited with establishing—especially for institutional and governmental buildings—what came to be known as the Second Empire style. The National Register of Historic Places notes, "The [early] date of its construction and the excellence of its architectural detail give this building a seminal position

16 **Vassar College.** One of Renwick's buildings that helped popularize the Second Empire style in the United States.

in the development in the United States of the Second Empire style, which achieved such wide popularity." Renwick soon designed two other buildings in this style: Charity Hospital (1858–61), on Blackwell's Island, and the main building on the campus of Vassar College (1861–65), both in New York (fig. 16). The style eventually swept the country in numerous governmental, commercial, and residential buildings, many featuring a prominent central tower, mansard roofs, quoins, and iron cresting. Buildings in the style reached gigantic proportions in the

17 State, War, and Navy Building.
This enormous building, also in the Second Empire style, was across Pennsylvania Avenue from the Corcoran Gallery.

Philadelphia City Hall (1871–1901), designed by John McArthur, and the State, War, and Navy Building (1871–88; now the Eisenhower Executive Office Building), across from Corcoran's gallery and designed by Alfred B. Mullett (fig. 17).

The War Begins

The Civil War brought a sea change to Washington and to the construction of Corcoran's gallery. Lincoln was elected president in November 1860, but before his inauguration in March 1861 seven states had seceded from the Union to form the Confederate States of America. Confederate forces attacked Fort Sumter in South Carolina in April, and war was declared (fig. 18). Many residents of Washington, located between the slave states of Virginia and Maryland, were Southern in their sympathies. Slavery was still legal in the District of Columbia. With the outbreak of war, however, hostility toward "seseches" (secessionist sympathizers) became virulent. Congress enacted a law requiring all federal employees to take an oath of allegiance to the US Constitution, resulting in charges being brought against 550 workers.

William Corcoran's Southern sympathies were well known. He had entertained prominent Southerners in his home and had managed their financial affairs, including those of Jefferson Davis, who would become president of the Confederacy in 1861. Corcoran himself had owned slaves, though he had freed them by 1856. He opposed the war, and believed "The South should have her rights in peace." With his blessing, Corcoran's daughter, Louise, in 1859 married George Eustis Jr., a young congressman from Louisiana, in the ballroom of Corcoran's home. The elaborate ceremony and reception were attended by some 1,500 guests.

18 **Fort Sumter, South Carolina.** The Confederates' capture of the fort marked the beginning of the Civil War.

HAY & STRAW DEPT COR. OF F & 18TH ST.

COCCORAN'S PRIVATE CLOTHING DEPT. ART BUILDING.

BEEF DEPOT MONUMENT.

GRAND CORRAL OR HORSE DEPOT, NEAR WASHINGTON, D. C., FOR THE REQUIREMENTS OF THE ARMY OF THE POTOMAC. GMU Libraries

158-155

19 **Civil War scenes in Washington.** Corcoran's unfinished gallery was confiscated by the Quartermaster Corps for a clothing depot at the beginning of the war.

In August 1861, following the Battle of Bull Run, in which the Union army suffered a humiliating defeat, Corcoran was arrested but quickly released, largely owing to the intervention of his friend Gideon Wells, secretary of the navy. But on August 19, Corcoran was notified in a letter from Secretary of War Simon Cameron that his gallery was being confiscated by the Quartermaster Corps for the war effort. The next day Corcoran, having no choice, replied through his agent that he was "willing that the Gvt should occupy the building as suggested in the Secy of War's letter," but that he expected rent to be paid.

Corcoran had written Renwick on April 10, 1861, that "in the present state of the country, nothing can be done and you will please therefore not press work further [on the building] until you hear from me." By that date the exterior was completed except for the figural sculptures and ornamental details. The interior, however, lacked flooring and plastering. The Quartermaster Corps would spend $2,500 finishing the interior to make it usable as a storage depot for uniforms and records (fig. 19).

A more serious and personal threat was made to seize Corcoran's residence on Lafayette Square. This disaster was averted when Corcoran rented the property to Henri Mercier, the French ambassador, for his official residence. Harewood, Corcoran's country estate, however, was confiscated for the construction of a military hospital complex (fig. 20).

Corcoran had endured enough. He liquidated as many of his ready assets as possible and placed them in the custody of his old friend George Peabody, who had been living in London since 1837. Then he sailed for Europe on October 8, 1862. Newspapers scornfully reported that he had taken $1.5 million out of the country with him, but this figure was an exaggeration. His destination was France. Corcoran's son-in-law, George Eustis, and his wife, Louise, had

20   **Harewood Hospital buildings.** Corcoran's country
estate was confiscated during the Civil War for this
complex of military hospital buildings. His stone villa
with cupola is visible in the distance at middle left.

traveled to Paris with the delegation that sought diplomatic recognition of the Confederacy by France. Although that effort failed, Eustis decided to remain in France in a villa near Cannes, where Corcoran joined them. Corcoran remained in Europe for the duration of the war, traveling, visiting friends, and collecting art.

General Meigs

The Civil War by 1863 was being fought on an enormous scale, and military support for it in Washington had expanded proportionally. The number of Union soldiers had increased from 17,000 at the beginning of the war to 310,000 three months later to two million by the end of the war. The personal staff in Washington of Quartermaster General Montgomery Meigs grew from 13 at the beginning of the war to 591 by war's end (fig. 21). Meigs wanted to consolidate his scattered offices and in October 1863 secured approval to relocate to Corcoran's gallery. Over the next three months he spent $30,000 to make alterations in the building suitable for his purposes. Galleries were partitioned into offices. A mezzanine was constructed in the main picture gallery on the second floor. A furnace and water closets were installed. The second floor was lit only by skylights, so the niches intended for sculpture on the outside of the building were converted into windows for more light (fig. 22). A separate two-story wooden annex was constructed behind the gallery. Meigs and his staff moved into the building in February 1864.

Montgomery Cunningham Meigs was born May 3, 1816, in Georgia, though he was brought up in Philadelphia. He was the oldest of 10 children born to Dr. Charles D. Meigs and Mary Montgomery Meigs. The family was of old New England stock, the first Meigses having settled in Connecticut in 1640. Meigs's father was a doctor and a professor of obstetrics and women's diseases at Philadelphia's Jefferson Medical College.

Montgomery was described by his mother as "high tempered, unyielding, tyrannical towards his brothers; very persevering in pursuit of anything he wishes; very inquisitive about the use of everything; delighted to see

21 Quartermaster General's staff.
The staff of General Montgomery Meigs grew rapidly as the Civil War progressed.

Corcoran's Art Building. –1861–6– U.S.Q.M. Dept. – Wash. D.C.

Corner of Penn. Ave. & 17th st cockt.

22 Corcoran Gallery building.
Union general Montgomery Meigs renovated the building for his headquarters during the Civil War.

different machines at work; appears to understand their different operation when explained to him." His ambition was to be an engineer.

After a year at the University of Pennsylvania, Meigs secured at age 16 an appointment to West Point through family influence. He excelled academically but accumulated almost the maximum allowable demerits for conduct. Later in life, he wrote that West Point's demerit system "pulled down the active, the enterprising, and put up at their expense the stolid, the namby pamby, the men having no distinguishing traits of character." He graduated fifth in his class, which ensured a commission as a second lieutenant in the army's elite Corps of Engineers.

For the next 14 years Meigs served at various posts around the country, working primarily on the construction of military fortifications. Notably, he was the assistant for a year to Captain Robert E. Lee in supervising improvements along the Mississippi River and the port at St. Louis. He married Louisa Rogers in 1841 and began to raise a family. In 1852 he was called to Washington, where he was promoted to captain and where he was to spend the remainder of his life.

Prior to the Civil War, Meigs ably handled a number of special assignments for then Secretary of War Jefferson Davis and others. During this period, he made two major contributions to the city. Washington badly needed a freshwater supply, having relied on wells and streams that could no longer meet the demand of the burgeoning population. Meigs proposed the construction of a massive 12-mile aqueduct system to bring water to the city from the unpolluted flow of the Potomac River above Great Falls. The most amazing feature of the project, which took 10 years and $2.4 million to complete, was Meigs's design and construction of the Aqueduct Bridge, still in use today as the Cabin John Bridge, which brought water over the then longest masonry arch in the world (fig. 23). The arch held that record for the next 40 years.

Meigs's other important involvement was with the construction of the House and Senate wings and the great cast-iron dome of the US Capitol. Architect Thomas U. Walter had won the

23	**Washington Aqueduct Bridge.** Meigs in 1853 designed this arch, which held the record for 40 years as the widest unsupported masonry arch in the world. Note the figures at bottom of photo.

competition for the design of these additions in 1851, but engineering and construction expertise and supervision from Meigs were needed to carry out this grand scheme. The strong personalities of the two men soon clashed, and vitriolic disputes ensued as to who had overriding authority for the implementation of the massive enterprise. Walter's design was followed, but Meigs made significant contributions to the structures and their decoration.

When war was declared in 1861, Meigs was still a captain. At the direction of Lincoln, Meigs had successfully participated in a special assignment to reinforce Fort Pickens in Florida. In operational planning conferences, he had impressed Lincoln with his clear thinking. Meigs's organizational ability, forthright manner, boundless energy, and impeccable honesty were widely recognized, though some detractors were concerned by his occasional arrogance. At six-foot-one and 200 pounds, he was an impressive figure. On June 13, 1861, Lincoln promoted Meigs to brigadier general and placed him in command of the army's Quartermaster Corps, commenting, "I do not know one who combines the qualities of masculine intellect, learning, and experience of the right sort, and physical power of labor and endurance, so well as he" (fig. 24).

The function of the Quartermaster Corps was to provide transportation, provisions, and other support for armies in the field. Railroads and ships were used whenever possible to carry men and goods in mass quantities, but wagons pulled by

24 **Montgomery Meigs.**
He was promoted to brigadier
general in 1861 to command
the Quartermaster Corps of
the Union army.

horses and mules were the backbone of supply lines for the frequent inland movement of troops. Each army had its own quartermaster, who reported to the commanding general and was responsible for local procurement of material, when that was possible. When local materials were not available, as was frequently the case, the Quartermaster General had to supply the necessary items, including horses for the cavalry, food for men and animals, uniforms, camp equipment, and medical supplies.

Meigs had to organize the logistics of this awesome operation from scratch. He regularly worked 12- to 14-hour days, establishing supply depots around the country to meet demand. By 1862, some 600 tons of supplies were being moved daily from the depots to advanced positions in the field. Wagons and horses were a constant challenge. Ideally, the requirement was one horse for every two men and one wagon for every 24 men. Toward the end of the war, the demand just for feeding the horses came to 2.5 million bushels of grain and 50,000 tons of hay each day. Expenditures by the Quartermaster Corps rose from $40,611,147 in 1861–62 to $284,809,697 by 1863–64. The cost of the war took a toll on the US Treasury never before experienced in the history of the country. Prior to the war, the national debt stood at $65 million; by the end of the war it was $2,678 million.

Meigs was constantly beset by problems, especially the corruption and fraud that were inevitable in the purchasing of such vast quantities of material. Meigs, sometimes aided by congressional investigations, tried whenever possible to expose it and stamp it out. He established a corps of inspectors who regularly visited operations in the field, as did Meigs himself when he could find the time. Another problem was the frequent turnover of personnel at his headquarters. Because promotions were limited for noncombatants, his men could always procure higher rank in the field. Despite the respect he commanded for his work, and much to his frustration, he remained a brigadier general until July 14, 1864, when he was finally promoted to brevet major general.

Meigs took one action that had lasting impact after the war. Because of its commanding position overlooking the Potomac, federal troops from the beginning of the war had occupied Arlington House, built by George Washington Parke Custis in 1818. Custis's only child, Mary Randolph Custis, had married Robert E. Lee in the mansion's parlor in 1831, and Arlington became their home, where six of their seven children were born. Upon her father's death in 1857, Mary inherited a life estate in the property, but she had fled in May 1861 with the threat of occupation by federal troops. In January 1864 the federal government, by somewhat dubious means, secured title to the property. Congress had earlier authorized the Quartermaster General to acquire land appropriate for the burial of Civil War dead. With ownership of Arlington House now in government hands, Meigs proposed to Secretary of War Edwin M. Stanton that the house and 200 acres surrounding it be set aside as a national military cemetery (fig. 25). Stanton concurred, and burials began immediately. The death of Meigs's eldest son in the war had deepened his bitterness toward the Confederates, especially West Point colleagues who had sided with the South, despite having taken the oath to support the US Constitution. He considered them traitors. He therefore directed that the burials be close to Arlington House, particularly in Mrs. Lee's rose garden, to prevent the Lee family from ever returning.

25 **Arlington House (Custis-Lee Mansion).** In 1864, General Meigs established Arlington National Cemetery on the mansion's grounds.

26 President Lincoln's death watch.
Meigs is the fifth figure from left, among cabinet members and Mrs. Lincoln.

After Lee's surrender at Appomattox came Lincoln's assassination on April 14, 1865. Meigs was among those who kept watch over the dying president throughout the night (fig. 26). In the following years, Meigs was kept busy transporting troops back home, disposing of the huge quantities of goods accumulated in the Quartermaster's storage depots, and reburying the Union dead in Arlington and other cemeteries.

Reclaiming the Gallery

With the conclusion of the war, Corcoran returned home from Europe in 1865, but the atmosphere was hostile to Southern sympathizers. Lincoln's assassination had precipitated universal outrage. Secretary of War Stanton had falsely claimed that the Confederacy was behind the murder and had offered a $100,000 reward for the capture of Confederate president Jefferson Davis. Corcoran promptly sailed back to Europe, but by 1867 the political climate had softened somewhat, and Corcoran finally returned to his Washington residence (fig. 27). His daughter, Louise Eustis, had died that year in France of tuberculosis, as her mother had before her, and Corcoran brought Louise's body back to be buried in the mausoleum he had erected at Oak Hill Cemetery. But despite the easing tensions, animosity toward him persisted. Secretary Stanton attempted to bring charges of tax evasion against him, but they were later dropped for lack of evidence.

Corcoran's gallery was still occupied by Meigs and the Quartermaster Corps in 1867. Corcoran's trusted agent and secretary, Anthony Hyde, who had managed his affairs in his absence, had repeatedly requested rent for the building, but to no avail. Corcoran's petitions for reclaiming the building did not bear fruit until May 10, 1869, when he was notified that the property would be restored to him. Corcoran immediately established a board of nine trustees to oversee the gallery. They included Hyde, his former banking partner George W. Riggs, Baltimore railroad magnate and art collector William T. Walters, and, later, Smithsonian secretary Joseph Henry. Corcoran then deeded the building to the trustees, along with an endowment of $900,000 for the acquisition of art and the operation of the

27   **William Corcoran.** Following his return from Europe after the Civil War, Corcoran was determined to regain his prominent position in the nation's capital. He had this portrait painted in 1867.

gallery. In his letter to the trustees, Corcoran stated his expectations for the new museum:

> *I venture to hope that with your kind co-operation and judicious management we shall have provided . . . not only a pure and refined pleasure for residents and visitors at the national metropolis, but have accomplished something useful in the development of American genius.*

Corcoran deliberately excluded himself from the board, though he periodically attended its meetings and inevitably influenced the gallery's direction over the succeeding years.

When the details of his munificent gift were reported in the newspapers, Corcoran was bombarded from all across the United States and abroad with offers to sell him "rare and valuable" works of art for the gallery, including many alleged old masters. All were declined. With the building now under their control, the trustees were able to press for back rent during occupancy by the Quartermaster Corps. After prolonged negotiations, Congress ultimately appropriated $125,000 in settlement of the claim, though Corcoran thought the amount should be $300,000.

Then, on May 24, 1870, the trustees succeeded in having the gallery chartered by Act of Congress, which made the museum tax-exempt. Thus, all the necessary actions were now complete to effect the "perpetual establishment and maintenance of a Public Gallery and Museum for the promotion and encouragement of the arts of painting and sculpture and the fine arts generally." The *Washington Daily Chronicle* emphasized the historic significance of Corcoran's gift as "in fact a national event. . . . The magnitude of this princely endowment will be better understood when we state that the edifice, which is shortly to contain choice specimens of American and foreign genius, is the only one in the United States expressly designed and constructed as a great art gallery. All the other collections in the leading cities are preserved in buildings intended for other purposes."

28 **Louise Home** (demolished). One of Corcoran's many charitable enterprises, it was built to house indigent Southern gentlewomen.

Corcoran had secured his gallery, but he now needed to re-establish his position of influence and importance in the nation's capital. He had a life-size portrait painted of himself that later hung in his gallery (see fig. 27), and he redoubled his philanthropic efforts. He contributed to the restoration of Mount Vernon. He donated land for a new building for the City Orphan Asylum, and served on its board of trustees. He contributed to a building for the newly formed YMCA. He donated to Columbian College (now George Washington University) a building for its medical school and 150 acres of land worth $250,000, and served as president of its board of trustees for 16 years. He built the Arlington Hotel, which in its day was one of the most fashionable hotels in the city, patronized by the likes of J. P. Morgan (see fig. 13 for location).

Nor did Corcoran neglect Southern causes. He constructed for $200,000 and endowed for $250,000 a residence for impoverished Southern gentlewomen, many of them widows of Confederate soldiers, and named it the Louise Home after his deceased wife and daughter (fig. 28). He contributed funds to Virginia colleges—William and Mary, Virginia Military Institute, Washington and Lee, and the University of Virginia—that had suffered during the war. He even presided over the Washington, DC, memorial service for Robert E. Lee in 1870.

Opening the Gallery

Simultaneously with these activities, Corcoran directed his efforts to refurbishing and opening his gallery (fig. 29). Fortuitously, on November 11, 1869, Edward Clark, Architect of the US Capitol, and Alfred B. Mullett, Supervising Architect of the Treasury Department, wrote to offer their services without compensation for the completion of the building:

> *Mr. Renwick has been compelled by business engagements to decline visiting this city to supervise the work. We are therefore willing to give our assistance in carrying out his designs, provided they are to be carried out in their entirety, as we think that his plans should be rigidly adhered to, and that the credit for the design and details should be entirely his.*

The offer was accepted immediately, and work began by local contractor William H. Falconer, who had been responsible for the construction of the building from the very beginning. The job included not only the removal of the alterations and additions made by the Quartermaster Corps but also the replacement of plastering, flooring, woodwork, and doors because the improvements made by the Quartermaster were not up to museum standards. The exterior niches for sculpture also had to be restored. As events developed, Edward Clark assumed primary oversight of the work, and he was subsequently elected a trustee of the gallery.

Finally, by 1871 the interior restoration was complete though not installed with art. Corcoran had a long-standing interest in the Washington Monument, which he referred to as "that chimney." Construction had been

29 **Main picture gallery (Grand Salon).** As the centerpiece of the gallery's opening in 1874, the main picture gallery featured paintings from Corcoran's collection, hung in the style of the day.

30   **President Ulysses Grant.**
He presided over a lavish ball
at the gallery before its official
opening and was a subsequent
visitor to the museum.

31   **William MacLeod.**
Appointed curator of the gallery
in 1873, he served in that capacity
for 16 years.

suspended in 1854 when private funding ceased. Corcoran agreed to chair
the newly created Joint Commission for the Completion of the Washington
Monument. He planned a grand ball with the dual purpose of celebrating
Washington's birthday and, more important, raising funds for the monument. The ball was held on February 20, 1871, in the gallery. Everybody
who was anybody attended: President and Mrs. Grant, Vice President
and Mrs. Colfax, the cabinet, General Sherman and other high-ranking
officers, members of Congress, the diplomatic corps, and prominent
citizens (fig. 30).

The entire building was decked with a profusion of flowers and evergreens, but the focus of the ball was the main picture gallery on the second floor lit by 285 gas jets from suspended pipes. Live canaries sang in cages hung from the ceiling. The presidential party was seated on a dais under a portrait of George Washington at the end of the room; portraits of Henry Clay, Andrew Jackson, Lincoln, and Grant adorned other walls. An orchestra played from a specially constructed balcony. The event was attended by 2,000 paying guests, but Corcoran was reported to have spent more of his own money on the gala than proceeds received for the monument. Washington and New York newspapers covered the event with lavish praise, hailing it as contributing to the city's rebirth. The ball clearly signaled Corcoran's reconciliation with the new order and his acceptance of and by the new Republican establishment. It also restored his preeminent social standing in the nation's capital.

Corcoran now needed to fill the building with art. In 1873 he deeded his art collection, valued at $100,000, to the gallery. That same year he sent trustee and collector William Walters, whose son later founded the Walters Art Museum in Baltimore, to Europe to buy art at Corcoran's expense. Walters had also moved to Europe during the Civil War and knew his way around the art world there. He purchased works by 19th-century artists popular at the time. He also arranged to buy plaster casts of the Elgin Marbles from the Parthenon frieze in the British Museum and replicas of the great bronze doors by Renaissance master Lorenzo Ghiberti from the Baptistery of San Giovanni in Florence. He acquired 60 bronze animal and other sculptures by noted French sculptor Antoine-Louis Barye. The trustees that same year hired William MacLeod as the first curator of the gallery, and he served in that capacity for the next 16 years (fig. 31). A native of Virginia, MacLeod had studied at the University of Glasgow and had become a painter of note. He relocated to Washington in 1854. Corcoran had purchased one of his paintings, *Great Falls of the Potomac.*

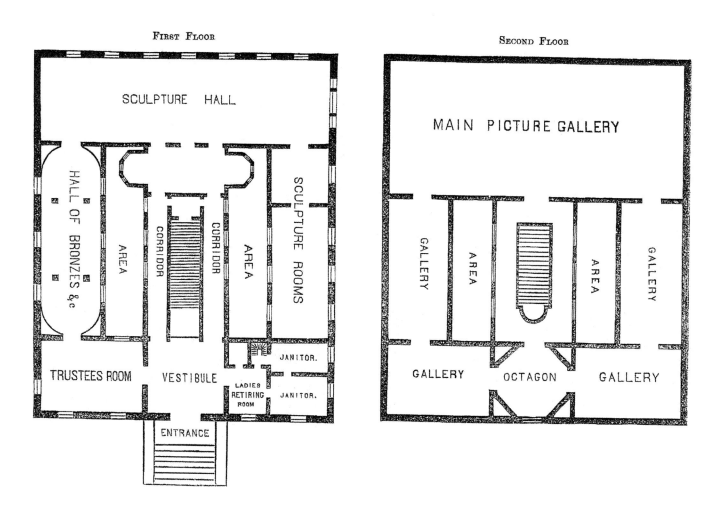

FIRST FLOOR

SECOND FLOOR

SCULPTURE HALL

HALL OF BRONZES &c

AREA

CORRIDOR

CORRIDOR

AREA

SCULPTURE ROOMS

TRUSTEES ROOM

VESTIBULE

LADIES RETIRING ROOM

JANITOR.

JANITOR.

ENTRANCE

MAIN PICTURE GALLERY

GALLERY

AREA

AREA

GALLERY

GALLERY

OCTAGON

GALLERY

32   Floor plans of the gallery.
This plan of the first and second floors was published in the gallery's first catalogue.

At last the Corcoran Gallery of Art opened to the public in 1874 in three stages. The first stage, in January, featured the Hall of Bronzes on the first floor with Barye sculptures; the Octagon Room on the second floor with *The Greek Slave* as its centerpiece; and the main picture gallery on the second floor, a magnificent space 95 feet long, 42 feet wide, and 38 feet high, painted

33 Hall of Bronzes. Some 60 small bronze figures by the French sculptor Antoine-Louis Barye were on view.

a plum color and hung from floor to ceiling salon-style with paintings from Corcoran's collection (see fig. 29; figs. 32–34). The 1867 life-size portrait of Corcoran was featured in the gallery (see fig. 27). President Grant stopped by on opening day for a visit. In April the Sculpture Hall at the rear of the first floor opened, featuring casts of the Parthenon frieze,

the baptistery doors, and casts of famous sculptures from antiquity, such as the Venus de Milo and the Apollo Belvedere (fig. 35). Curator MacLeod had a supply of fig leaves, so visitors "were carefully shielded from any 'offensive' anatomical elements." In December the rest of the building opened. There were a total of 350 works of art on display, of which 112 were paintings. The artworks had no labels or wall text; visitors had to buy a catalogue for 25 cents for information on the art and artists. The museum was open, also at a charge of 25 cents, on Mondays, Wednesdays, and Fridays, but was free on the other days except Sundays, when it was closed.

The press and public were enthusiastic in their praise of the gallery. The *New York Times* called the museum "a benefaction to the whole country . . . a Gallery of Fine Arts which will rival the most famous collections in the world." Indeed, the museum soon became known as the national art gallery: "Washington may now pride herself upon a National Art Gallery," proclaimed one journalist. The Smithsonian's Board of Regents considered the gallery "an important means of improving the intellectual and moral condition of the citizens

34 *The Greek Slave.* This famous sculpture by Hiram Powers was the prized work of Corcoran's collection and later the centerpiece of the gallery's Octagon Room.

35 **Sculpture Hall.** The Parthenon frieze runs below the ceiling, with the Apollo Belvedere at the end of the room, all plaster casts commissioned for the gallery.

of Washington." An even higher encomium compared the new museum to the Louvre. The *Philadelphia Bulletin*, in an article titled "Have We a Louvre among Us?," concluded that the gallery would indeed "make a highly creditable Louvre." Influential senator Charles Sumner agreed: "Senator Sumner, who takes a natural pride in the extension and decoration of his country's capital, bestows the title the *American Louvre* upon this new gallery," wrote one reporter. Comments about the art collection itself, however, were not universally favorable. A critic for *Century Illustrated Magazine* wrote in 1882: "Some of the pictures are of a quality so inferior to the best of the collection that one is surprised to find them there."

Attendance increased steadily after the gallery's opening, from 66,000 in the first year to 100,000 in 1878. By contrast, the Metropolitan Museum of Art in New York had only 42,000 visitors at that time. Guidebooks to Washington in this era noted that the Corcoran Gallery was the second most popular tourist destination after the Smithsonian but before the Washington Monument. The collection also grew in quantity and quality, with continued emphasis on American art. The $50,000 annual income from Corcoran's endowment ensured that new acquisitions were possible. A major addition in 1876 was the purchase for $12,500 of Frederic Church's monumental painting of Niagara Falls, then the highest price paid for a work by a living American artist. Corcoran wanted the collection also to present American history with "portraits of national heroes." Toward that goal, the trustees, between 1874 and 1885, purchased portraits of all the US presidents.

Noted artists of the day visited the gallery, including Thomas Moran, Asher Durand, and Sanford Gifford. Other visitors were more unusual. In 1880 a delegation of Apache Indians came to town to negotiate a treaty. They visited the gallery in Western clothes, but Curator MacLeod wanted a photograph of them in native dress, so they returned the next day with an Anglo agent and interpreter and were duly photographed in front of Church's *Niagara* (fig. 36).

DELEGATION OF JICARILLA APACHE INDIANS, VISITING THE CORCORAN GALLERY OF ART, APRIL 2, 1880.

Dr. BENJ. THOMAS, Agent.

SANTIAGO LARGO,   AUGUSTINE.   HUERITO,   Mr. ALEX. READ,
(JAMES LONG.)   (LITTLE BLOND.)   Interpreter.

36   Indian delegation visiting the gallery.
The Apaches had come to Washington
to negotiate a treaty.

The Later Years

The 1880s saw the execution of the missing sculptural decoration on the exterior of the gallery. Moses Ezekiel was a Richmond native who had attended the Virginia Military Institute and had fought for the Confederacy in the Civil War, a fact that appealed to Corcoran. Ezekiel later studied sculpture in Berlin and maintained a studio for 30 years in the ruins of the Baths of Diocletian in Rome. Corcoran, who had earlier known Ezekiel and had showed him around the gallery, commissioned sculptures from him to fill the 11 vacant niches on the front and side of the building. From 1879 to 1884, Ezekiel produced, in white Carrara marble, statues seven feet high representing the world's famous artists, as selected by the gallery's trustees with input from Corcoran. The price was $650 for each figure, to be paid as the statues, each weighing 1,500 pounds, were completed and shipped from Rome to Washington. On the front facade were installed Phidias, Raphael, Michelangelo, and Dürer (fig. 37). On the side of the building were placed Titian, Leonardo, Rubens, Rembrandt, Murillo, Canova, and the American sculptor Thomas Crawford, who had lived and died in Rome and had been a friend of Ezekiel's. Crawford's most famous work is *Freedom*, the 19½-foot-high bronze statue crowning the dome of the US Capitol.

James Renwick had designated the triangular tympanum above the building's central pavilion for a sculptural group representing "the genius of art," but the trustees instead commissioned Ezekiel to produce a bronze medallion profile portrait of Corcoran within a wreath (fig. 38). To ensure that the portrayal was accurate, Corcoran had a profile photograph taken of himself, which he sent to Ezekiel. The drawing Ezekiel returned did not

37 **Corcoran Gallery.** Eleven marble sculptures representing the world's famous artists were installed on the facade.

38 Profile bronze of Corcoran. His visage was sculpted by Moses Ezekiel for the building's facade from a photograph provided by Corcoran.

39 Corcoran's initials. "WWC" was mounted in bronze as a decorative element on the building's facade.

40 Corncob capitals. As an American touch, Renwick incorporated corncobs among the acanthus leaves in his capitals.

please Corcoran: "The general expression amounting to a scowl is neither what my friends or myself desire." He sent another photograph, but this time he approved the revised sketch. On each of the pavilions, Corcoran's bronze initials, "WWC," were mounted in roundels under sculpted swags (fig. 39). Renwick's corncob capitals are clearly shown here (fig. 40).

A final sculptural enhancement came in 1888 with the purchase for $1,900 of a pair of life-size bronze lions—one asleep and one half-asleep—to flank the front entrance (fig. 41). They were copies of marble originals carved by Italian sculptor Antonio Canova in 1792 for the cenotaph of Pope Clement XIII. A final program for the gallery's interior

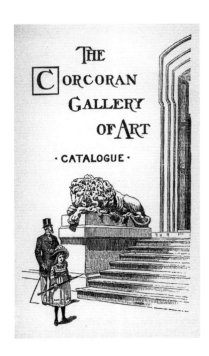

41 **Corcoran Gallery catalogue.**
This 1892 cover illustration depicts one of the bronze lions at the gallery's entrance.

42 **Decoration of the Grand Salon.**
This decorative scheme in the frieze was later painted over and lost.

decoration focused on the main picture gallery. Upon the recommendation of artist Albert Bierstadt, the trustees hired New York decorator Vincent G. Stiepevich to paint the coved frieze of this gallery with idealized portrait busts of famous artists in oval medallions interspersed amid stylized scrolls (fig. 42). Much of the work was done by Stiepevich's

43 **Students visiting the gallery.**
An art school was established in a separate building behind the gallery in 1890.

studio assistants in 36 days in 1880 at a cost of $1,870.

Education, or "encouraging American genius" as he phrased it, was one of Corcoran's founding principles in creating his gallery of art. He had contributed funds to establish an art school to be associated with the gallery, but he did not live to see it realized. The trustees did fulfill his intent, however, when in 1889 they constructed a building for the art school, designed by Edward Clark and located behind the gallery where the Quartermaster Corps' annex once stood. The school opened in 1890 with a principal in charge, three classrooms, and a large gallery lit by skylights for life classes. The school was an immediate success (fig. 43). In that same year electric lighting was introduced in the galleries of the main building.

As the collection expanded dramatically over time and the need for special exhibition space emerged, the museum outgrew the confines of the original building. Corcoran had attempted to buy the vacant lot north of the museum's property, but the owner adamantly refused to sell. The trustees decided to relocate and in 1891 purchased property on 17th Street three blocks south of the gallery. An architectural competition was held for the design of the new building and was won by 35-year-old Ernest Flagg of New York City. His Beaux-Arts edifice, which was in stark contrast to Renwick's Victorian structure, was intended to incorporate the most advanced museum design in the United States at the time

44 **The new Corcoran Gallery of Art.** The gallery moved to this Beaux-Arts building in 1897 after the collection and staff outgrew the earlier building.

(fig. 44). The new museum opened in 1897 with a grand reception attended by 3,000 guests, including President Cleveland and his cabinet. By that date the museum's collection numbered 1,856 works of art.

✻ ✻ ✻ ✻ ✻

William Corcoran was described in his golden years as "scrupulously neat in his person, [who] carried a gold-headed cane, and wore gloves in the street, but was entirely devoid of affectation or vanity. . . . He always retained an old-fashioned courtesy of manner . . . and was not surpassed

MILLIONAIRES OF THE UNITED STATES.

45 **Millionaires of the United States in 1884.** Corcoran (bottom row, second from left) is among the 15 millionaires illustrated here. See Notes (p. 101) for a list of the other millionaires depicted.

46 **William Corcoran at home.** In retirement he is relaxing in the library of his mansion.

as a raconteur." He continued to make investments, especially in land. He owned property in states as dispersed as Washington, Oregon, Michigan, Illinois, Mississippi, Texas, and New York. In 1884 he was one of 15 millionaires in the United States, along with Cornelius Vanderbilt, William Waldorf Astor, Jay Gould, and Leland Stanford (fig. 45).

Corcoran continued buying art for the gallery and supporting philanthropic causes to the end of his life (fig. 46). He donated 36,000 acres to the Episcopal Diocese of Texas and 11,000 acres to the Episcopal Diocese of Mississippi. He even gave modest donations to individuals in distress. In his last year, Corcoran was receiving as many as 50 begging letters each day. His secretary, Anthony Hyde, in exasperation devised

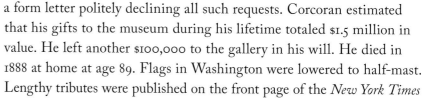

47　**Corcoran's tomb.** He was buried in Oak Hill Cemetery in 1888 beside his wife, daughter, and son-in-law.

a form letter politely declining all such requests. Corcoran estimated that his gifts to the museum during his lifetime totaled $1.5 million in value. He left another $100,000 to the gallery in his will. He died in 1888 at home at age 89. Flags in Washington were lowered to half-mast. Lengthy tributes were published on the front page of the *New York Times* and the *Washington Post*, praising him as "the first citizen of the District of Columbia." He was laid to rest in his marble temple in Oak Hill Cemetery beside his wife, daughter, and son-in-law (fig. 47).

James Renwick designed one final building for William Corcoran after the Civil War. It was a large six-story commercial building, completed in 1876 and located across the street from the east side of the US Treasury Building (see fig. 13 for location). Renwick continued his prolific architectural practice in a career that eventually spanned a remarkable 52 years. At over six feet tall, he cut an imposing figure and moved in the most fashionable circles of New York. He was described as wellborn, cultivated, and a gourmet (fig. 48). His buildings in his later decades included residences for affluent friends and patrons, numerous churches, commercial buildings, a theater, and a YMCA, mostly in New York and in

48 James Renwick. His prolific architectural practice extended over a period of 52 years.

historicist styles. He grew wealthy, both from his own earnings and from his wife's inheritance, and maintained two steam yachts, one near his home and the other in Florida for tarpon fishing. He traveled to Europe every two years and collected old-master paintings and decorative arts.

He died in 1895 at age 76 and was buried beside his wife in Green-Wood Cemetery in Brooklyn. Renwick bequeathed a bust of himself and his collection of 74 artworks to the Metropolitan Museum of Art in New York with the condition that the entire collection be displayed with his bust in a special room to be known as the James Renwick Collection. The bequest was declined.

Montgomery Meigs retired from the army in 1882, but he was not idle in his later years (fig. 49). He had been and continued to be an active member of the National Academy of Sciences, and in 1885 he was elected to the Smithsonian's Board of Regents. His final architectural achievement was the design and construction of the Pension Building (now the National Building Museum) in Washington, erected 1882–87 to process pensions for Civil War veterans (fig. 50). The structure encompassed an enormous interior courtyard, which instantly became

49 **Montgomery Meigs.** He was promoted to brevet major general in 1864 and retired in 1882.

50 **Pension Building.** Meigs's last project was this building for the processing of Civil War pensions.

the favorite venue for presidents' inaugural balls. The structure's striking architectural ornament was a terra-cotta frieze three feet high encircling the building, depicting various military units of the Civil War. Constructed of 15.5 million bricks, the building was sometimes referred to as "Meigs' red brick barn." Meigs died at home in 1892 at age 75 and was entombed in a marble sarcophagus beside his wife and son in Grave Site No. 1 at Arlington National Cemetery.

The Court of Claims

After the Corcoran Gallery vacated the building, the trustees rented it to the federal government for use by the Court of Claims, which initially stored records on the first floor. Then in 1901 the government bought the building for $300,000 as the permanent home for the court, which had earlier been located in such places as the Willard Hotel and the US Capitol (fig. 51). At the same time, the 11 Ezekiel sculptures were removed from the facade and sold to private buyers. Evalyn Walsh McLean, owner of the Hope Diamond, purchased six of them to decorate the swimming pool at her suburban home, Friendship (now the site of the residential complex McLean Gardens). Decades later, eight of the statues were donated to the Norfolk Botanical Gardens in Virginia, where they remain today (fig. 52). The pair of bronze lions had gone to the new Corcoran Gallery of Art, where they continue to grace the building's entrance.

The Court of Claims had been established in 1855 by Act of Congress. Before then, monetary claims brought against the federal government had to be submitted to Congress by petition, but this process had become burdensome and unworkable. The court was granted authority to adjudicate all monetary claims based upon a law, a regulation, or a government contract, with appeal to the US Supreme Court. Because the court was the tribunal to which citizens could bring lawsuits against their government, it was sometimes called "the people's court" and "the keeper of the nation's conscience." The court initially had three judges, who were granted lifetime appointments and were authorized to appoint commissioners to investigate claims, issue subpoenas, and take depositions.

51 **Courtroom of the Court of Claims.** Half of the Corcoran Gallery's Grand Salon became a courtroom in 1901.

52 *Leonardo da Vinci.* This marble statue, once displayed on the gallery's facade, ended up in the Norfolk Botanical Gardens in Virginia.

To accommodate its functions and to introduce modern conveniences, the court over the years made many changes to the building. The main picture gallery (Grand Salon) on the second floor was divided into a courtroom on one side (see fig. 51) and a docket room on the other (fig. 53). Elevators were installed, along with a revolving door at the front entrance. Windows were opened on the second floor where niches had held the Ezekiel sculptures, and the skylights on that floor were closed. Fluorescent hanging lights were another modern innovation. Restroom facilities and the heating plant were upgraded.

As the volume of cases coming before the court increased over the years, the number of the judges also increased, first to five, then to seven, then to fifteen. The monetary total of the judgments rendered by the court each year also increased dramatically. Inevitably, the court's name, procedures, and

53 **Entrance to the Docket Room.**
The other half of the Grand Salon
served as a docket room for the
inspection of court records.

jurisdiction changed over the decades (fig. 54). Most of the cases brought before the court involved government contracts and tax disputes, although the court also had jurisdiction over Indian claims.

As early as 1931 the court complained of lack of space. A scheme to enlarge the building by adding to the rear was not realized. The galleries and the two light courts were eventually partitioned into a warren of offices. Another continuing problem involved the ornamental sandstone trim on the building's two primary facades. The stone began to spall and fall off as early as 1903. Repairs were periodically made, but the deterioration continued. The building suffered an unfortunate loss during World War II when the metal cresting on the roof was removed and donated to the national scrap-metal drive to be melted down for the war effort. Also during the war, President Roosevelt ordered wooden mock-ups of machine guns to be mounted on the roof to deter possible attacks on the White House. The art school building behind the gallery was converted into a parking garage for Court of Claims personnel (fig. 55).

54 **Pennsylvania Avenue parade.** The Court of Claims (former Corcoran Gallery building) is at lower right; the State, War, and Navy Building is at lower left.

55 **Parking garage.** The former art school building behind the gallery was converted into a garage.

Victorian architecture was at this time scorned as unnecessarily fussy, stylistically derivative, and a prime candidate for demolition. William Corcoran's mansion on the north side of Lafayette Square had been demolished in 1922 and replaced by the current US Chamber of Commerce Building. By 1956, Chief Justice Marvin Jones of the Court of Claims was urging that the old gallery building be demolished and a new structure suitable to the court's needs erected on the site. He complained that the building was a fire hazard, that it was in poor condition (especially the rear annex), that the building's systems were hopelessly antiquated, and that the 20- to 38-foot ceilings were a waste of space that made the building difficult to heat (fig. 56). He particularly cited the badly deteriorated stone on the facade, which by this time was falling in pieces on the sidewalks below and endangering pedestrians. A bill was introduced in Congress by his friend Senator Lyndon Johnson to demolish and replace the building. The bill failed in committee, however, when, among others in opposition, David E. Finley, chairman of the US Commission of Fine Arts, argued that the building should be retained and the court should move to a location near the Supreme Court or other federal courts. As the former director of Washington's National Gallery of Art and chairman of the National Trust for Historic Preservation, Finley carried considerable influence.

An even greater need for additional space had arisen when the many agencies, offices, and staff personnel reporting to the president had outgrown the old State, War, and Navy Building, renamed the Executive Office Building, which was across the street from the Court of Claims. To solve this problem, the General Services Administration asked two respected Boston architectural firms to submit proposals for new federal office buildings on Lafayette Square that would also house the Court of Claims. The resulting plan called for outsize modern buildings on the east and west sides of the square, which would require the demolition of many historic 19th-century structures as well as the Court of Claims building.

56 Building as Court of Claims.
The building by the 1950s was in poor condition, as seen in this rear view. The metal cresting on the roof had been removed for scrap during World War II.

After some requested modifications were made, the project was approved in 1961 with reservations by President Kennedy and by a narrow vote of the Commission of Fine Arts, with Chairman Finley vociferously dissenting. The plan proposed the creation of a park on the site of the former Corcoran Gallery.

Saving the Building

As an undergraduate, Jacqueline Bouvier Kennedy had spent her junior year in France and greatly admired its architecture. She was sophisticated and cultured in history and the arts. Even before she became First Lady, she "knew that the White House would be one of my main projects if he [Jack] won," she recalled in a 1961 interview for *Life* magazine. The furniture in the White House at the time was largely from the Truman years, when the mansion had been gutted, reconstructed, and furnished primarily with reproductions from the Kittinger firm of New York. Mrs. Kennedy began by establishing the White House Fine Arts Committee as an advisory body and appointing David Finley to it. Upon her completion of the redecoration, CBS News produced the program "A Tour of the White House with Mrs. John F. Kennedy," which was broadcast February 14, 1962, to an estimated 56 million viewers.

But Mrs. Kennedy was also concerned about the proposed development across from the White House. She had seen the plans for the massive new buildings on Lafayette Square and thought they were a disaster. She invited David Finley, who was married to Corcoran's great-granddaughter, to give her a tour of the square the day after the television broadcast, and asked him what she could do to stop or modify the plans, including the proposed demolition of the old Corcoran Gallery (fig. 57). Upon Finley's advice, on March 6, 1962, she wrote to Bernard L. Boutin, head of the General Services Administration, who had the final word on the project. In her letter she noted that it was important to the president that the plan be well done, and that the oversize modern buildings were totally out of character in scale and

57 **David Finley with President and Mrs. Kennedy.** In 1962, Jacqueline Kennedy and David Finley (at microphones), chairman of the Commission of Fine Arts, were instrumental in saving the gallery from demolition.

materials with the historic square. She further made an eloquent plea to retain the old Corcoran building:

> *It may look like a Victorian horror, but it is really quite a lovely and precious example of the period of architecture which is fast disappearing. I so strongly feel that the White House should give the example in preserving our nation's past. Now we think of saving old buildings like Mount Vernon and tear down everything in the 19th Century—but, in the next hundred years, the 19th Century will be of great interest and there will [be] none of it left. . . . The Fine Arts Commission and the architects want to tear this down and put a park in its place because they think it makes the block symmetrical. I hope you will use all of your influence to see that this building is preserved and not replaced with a few trees. We also have received a great deal of mail on the subject of this building.*

She went on to suggest possible alternative uses for the building, including an art museum. The letter worked. Boutin responded that he would make every effort to fulfill her and the president's wishes.

Coincidentally, San Francisco architect John Carl Warnecke was in Washington the following month to judge an architectural competition. His old friend Paul Fay, undersecretary of the navy, invited him to come along to the White House for a reunion of "PT-boat heroes" with President Kennedy. Warnecke, not an invited guest of the reunion, was told to be careful not to be photographed with any of the heroes. He did speak to the president, who had met him when he was a star Stanford football player. The next day, at a dinner with the president, Fay explained that Warnecke was now a highly respected architect known for his contextual architecture and might be of assistance in resolving the planning problems of Lafayette Square. The president took this advice and later invited Warnecke to meet with him to discuss a possible solution. Warnecke believed that "the old buildings . . . are a symbol of the White House and a symbol of America.

They should all be kept, as many as you can keep. . . . Make the historic buildings be an important part of the project." In his meeting with Kennedy, Warnecke proposed an earlier alternative, which was to place the large new government buildings behind the historic structures so that the scale of Lafayette Square would be preserved; the government buildings would face other streets. Kennedy immediately approved the concept. Within weeks Boutin terminated the contract with the two Boston architectural firms and hired Warnecke to take charge of the project. Warnecke commissioned a feasibility study to demonstrate that the buildings on the square could be rehabilitated for new purposes. His plans were endorsed enthusiastically by Jacqueline Kennedy, who had been away on a trip to India, but not quite as enthusiastically by the Fine Arts Commission; one architect on the commission who had held out for "modern architecture" sniped in defeat, "I just hope Jacqueline wakes up to the fact that she lives in the twentieth century" (fig. 58). The Court of Claims moved out of the former Corcoran Gallery to temporary quarters in 1964, and later, somewhat ironically, into restored historic buildings on the east side of Lafayette Square. The Corcoran building had been saved, but its future purpose had not been decided.

58 **Jacqueline Kennedy and architect John Carl Warnecke.** They are reviewing a model for the restoration of Lafayette Square and retention of the Corcoran Gallery building.

RENWICK GALLERY

HAS BEEN DESIGNATED A

REGISTERED NATIONAL
HISTORIC LANDMARK

UNDER THE PROVISIONS OF THE
HISTORIC SITES ACT OF AUGUST 21, 1935
THIS SITE POSSESSES EXCEPTIONAL VALUE
IN COMMEMORATING OR ILLUSTRATING
THE HISTORY OF THE UNITED STATES

U. S. DEPARTMENT OF THE INTERIOR
NATIONAL PARK SERVICE

1972

Restoring the Building

S. Dillon Ripley became the eighth Secretary of the Smithsonian Institution in 1964. Imaginative, energetic, and resourceful, he set as his goal the expansion of the institution in new directions. Under his guidance, the Smithsonian would eventually open six new museums, establish a national membership program, publish an attractive magazine, and create an annual folk life festival, among other accomplishments. But his current focus was on the vacant Corcoran Gallery building, whose future was in limbo. On May 27, 1965, he invited President Lyndon Johnson to tour the building with him. Now that it had been saved, Johnson took a new interest in its future possibilities as a place where distinguished foreign visitors, who were usually lodged next door at Blair House, the president's official guest residence, could hold conferences and meetings. Instead, Ripley proposed that the building be renovated as a museum or gallery under the Smithsonian and that it could display American decorative and folk art, with temporary exhibitions of the arts and crafts of the country of the head of state visiting next door. Johnson liked this idea, and on June 23 wrote to Ripley:

> *I am enthusiastic about your suggestions that the Smithsonian Institution take over the old U.S. Court of Claims Building and establish it as a gallery of arts, crafts and design. No more appropriate purpose for the building could be proposed than to exhibit, in the restored gallery, examples of the ingenuity of our people and to present exhibits from other nations, whose citizens are so proud of their arts. . . . I . . . am therefore instructing Mr. Lawson Knott, Administrator of the General Services Administration, to transfer the building to the Smithsonian Institution.*

59 **A National Historic Landmark.** Smithsonian secretary S. Dillon Ripley (right) and Nathaniel Reed, assistant secretary of the Department of the Interior, unveil the plaque designating the restored building a National Historic Landmark, May 4, 1973.

60 *Murillo.* This sculpture of the Spanish artist was replicated from the original in the Norfolk Botanical Gardens and installed on the building's restored facade.

The transfer was accomplished on July 20, 1965, and funds were appropriated for the building's restoration, the cost of which ultimately totaled $2.6 million. John Carl Warnecke and Associates as supervising architects was tasked with the overall renovation, with Universal Restorations of Washington, DC, in charge of the building's exterior restoration. The gallery and its programs were to be administered as a curatorial department of the Smithsonian's National Collection of Fine Arts (now the Smithsonian American Art Museum). David Scott, that museum's director, recommended that the building be named the Renwick Gallery in honor of its architect, and Ripley concurred.

A thorough overhaul of the building was required. Work began in 1967 and was not completed until 1972. The immediate task was the underpinning and shoring up of the building's north wall, which was on the verge of collapse. The partitions inserted by the Court of Claims were removed, and the original gallery plan of the building was restored. Completely new plumbing, wiring, lighting, elevators, heating and cooling, and other systems were installed. The metal cresting on the roof was replicated and replaced in aluminum using old photographs and original metal scraps found on the roof. A more challenging problem was the badly eroded sandstone that comprised approximately 25 percent of the two primary facades. The solution was to make the repairs with Dekosit, a patented material composed of crushed stone in a latex binder. The final touch on the exterior was to place sculptures in two niches on the building's west facade. The sculptor Renato Lucchetti was commissioned to replicate the figures of Rubens and Murillo for the niches. The statues were made of a conglomerate marble dust from molds of the originals in the Norfolk Botanical Gardens, and were installed in 1974 (fig. 60).

Local architect Hugh Newell Jacobsen was hired to transform the interior of the building. He decided to refurbish the main picture

61 Hanging paintings in the Grand Salon. Staff members Lloyd Herman (right) and Harry Lowe supervise preparations for the gallery's opening. Herman holds an image (ca. 1880) of the Grand Salon (see fig. 29).

62 (Overleaf) **Grand Salon.** Paintings were hung salon-style, with a number of the same works that had been displayed in the gallery in the 19th century.

63 (Overleaf) **Octagon Room.** Custom-woven draperies graced this restored gallery, which once featured *The Greek Slave.*

gallery (renamed the Grand Salon) and the Octagon Room as opulent period rooms intended to evoke the Victorian world in which Renwick had lived. He commissioned a custom-designed fabric from Old World Weavers of New York for draperies in the two rooms. The Grand Salon was painted its original plum color and was hung 19th-century style with American paintings from the National Collection of Fine Arts and paintings borrowed from the Corcoran Gallery of Art that had originally hung in the room (figs. 61–63). Once again, a life-size portrait of William Corcoran was prominently featured. Unfortunately, the decorative painting in the frieze by Stiepevich had been so damaged that it could not be recovered. The other galleries were restored but painted white for changing exhibitions and the display of objects.

89 · RESTORING THE BUILDING

The Renwick Today

*L*loyd E. Herman in 1971 was appointed administrator and later director of the Renwick Gallery (see fig. 61). He had been the director of programs for the Smithsonian's Arts and Industries Building, adjacent to the Castle. He immediately set about developing exhibitions to open the gallery that would reflect its mission of presenting the best of American crafts and design. He organized eight exhibitions that covered such diverse subjects as Craftsman furniture and glass, design renderings, historic objects, and Indian pottery. The gallery opened January 26, 1972, with the first of three black-tie receptions attended by distinguished representatives of the political, diplomatic, arts, and social communities of Washington, including President and Mrs. Nixon, Chief Justice and Mrs. Burger, and Alice Roosevelt Longworth (fig. 64).

The restoration and opening of the Renwick Gallery were national news. Large and small newspapers across the country—from Pomona, California, to Nashua, New Hampshire—carried the story. Ada Louise Huxtable, architecture critic for the *New York Times,* praised the interior restoration as "getting it back to the spirit of Renwick," rather than seeking a literal reproduction. The *Washington Post* concluded: "[The restoration] is a triumph of American culture over the spiteful neglect with which we treat our cities." The American Institute of Architects in 1974 recognized John Warnecke and Hugh Jacobsen for their achievement with an award, which proclaimed: "The Renwick Gallery restoration is a masterpiece of creative preservation, a lesson which should be applied in every town and city in the country which

64 **Grand stairway.** Visitors were invited upstairs to the main galleries by this impressive staircase.

has older buildings which should be kept and used." The importance of the building had been officially recognized earlier when it was listed on the National Register of Historic Places in 1969 and designated a National Historic Landmark in 1972 (see fig. 59).

Only three years after the Renwick's opening, it became clear that the Dekosit repairs on the facade's sandstone did not solve the problem; large pieces of stone were delaminating and falling off the building (fig. 65). The situation became so hazardous that wooden shelters were erected over the sidewalks to shield pedestrians from falling debris. The Smithsonian undertook an extensive study of the problem, including the search for a matching stone, but concluded that the best permanent solution was to remove all of the sandstone and replace it with a special concrete mix tinted and cast from molds to match

65 **Deteriorating stone on facade.** Earlier attempts to remedy this increasingly serious problem had failed.

66 Removal of stone on facade.
Deteriorating stone elements were finally removed and replaced with concrete aggregate replicated from exact molds.

the original architectural elements (fig. 66). This did finally solve the problem (fig. 67).

The Renwick Gallery opened without a collection, but craft artists and others soon began to offer donations. Contemporary crafts were an entirely new area of collecting for museums at the time, and

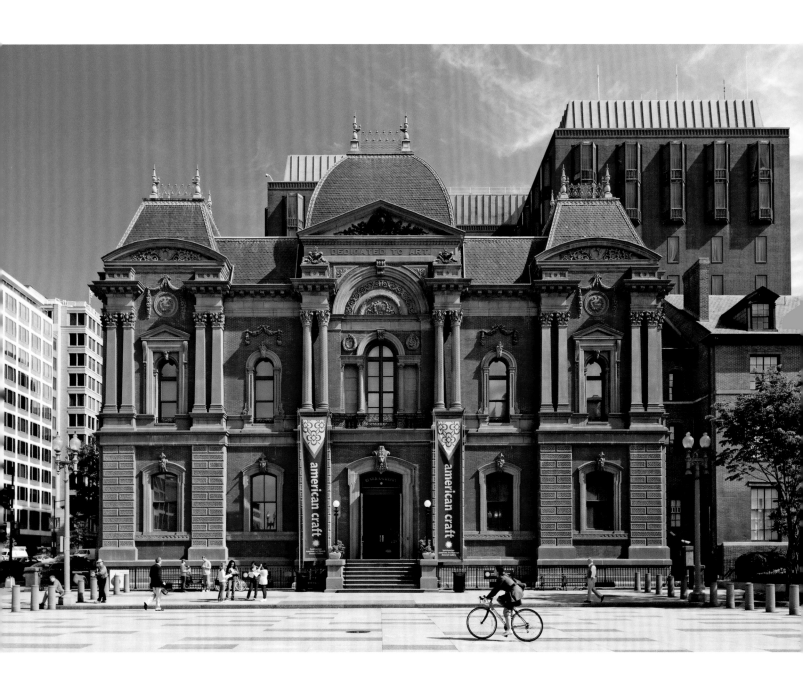

67 **Renwick Gallery.** After its 1967–72 restoration and later stone repairs, the gallery stood ready to delight visitors for the coming decades.

68 **Paley Gates.** The gates were commissioned from Albert Paley in 1974 for the entrance of the gallery's gift shop.

Lloyd Herman went to great lengths to seek out and recognize the best craftsmen. Toward this goal, Herman announced a competition for the design of entrance gates to the gallery's gift shop. The winner was 31-year-old Albert Paley. The gates, installed in 1976 and widely published since then, launched Paley's national career (fig. 68). The founding of the Renwick Alliance in 1982 as a support group for the gallery greatly enhanced both its collection and its programs.

At the beginning, the Renwick did mount exhibitions of the arts and crafts of other nations, although it proved impossible to time such exhibitions with the visits of foreign heads of state. With the renaming of its parent museum as the National Museum of American Art in 1980, the Renwick focused its collecting on post–World War II American crafts and its exhibitions on American decorative arts and craft objects. The gallery's staff and collection increased substantially over the years. The collection now numbers 2,035 objects and includes the work of such acclaimed craft artists as Anni Albers, Wendell Castle, Dale Chihuly, and Peter Voulkos.

69 Gallery under renovation. An extensive renovation and upgrade of the building were undertaken in 2013–15.

And in recent years the gallery has examined evolving notions of craft through the work of a new generation of practitioners in fields as diverse as industrial and fashion design, as well as sustainable manufacturing. Today the Renwick is widely recognized as one of the nation's premier venues for the collecting, exhibiting, and publishing of American crafts.

In 2013 a two-year, $30 million renovation of the venerable building began under the supervision of the architectural firm Westlake Reed Leskosky (fig. 69). The systems installed during the Renwick's restoration 50 years earlier had outlived their useful life and needed to be updated. This latest renovation included the replacement of all heating, air conditioning, electrical, plumbing, and fire-suppression systems, as well as upgrades to security and communications, with wireless Internet access throughout the building. The original window configurations have been re-created and the basement redesigned for improved staff offices and workshops. Perhaps the most dramatic change has been the restoration of the original vaulted ceilings in two galleries on the second floor (fig. 70), and the

70   **Restoration of ceilings.** An original
vaulted ceiling, shown above the
1960s dropped ceiling before
renovation, was restored in this
and one other second-floor gallery.

71 **Renwick Gallery pediment.**
The building has come full circle
to its original purpose.

Renwick now features LED lighting systems, dramatically enhancing its energy efficiency.

The Corcoran Gallery of Art was a cultural pioneer in the nation's capital, and in its two buildings was the only art museum in the city for 50 years. It paved the way for the plethora of subsequent museums, including the Phillips Collection, which opened in 1921; the Freer Gallery of Art, which opened in 1923; and the National Gallery of Art, which opened in 1941. The original Corcoran building and the Old Patent Office Building, which houses the Renwick's parent museum, the Smithsonian American Art Museum, were under construction at the same time in the 19th century but in entirely different architectural styles, one to serve the American genius of art, the other to serve the American genius of invention and technology. Both buildings were renovated in the 1960s for art museum use. It is fitting that they are now joined in common endeavor.

The Renwick Gallery building has survived wartime expropriation, abuse and neglect, and threatened demolition over its 160-year history. It has been subject to many changes and challenges but has come full circle to serve its original purpose, "Dedicated to Art" (fig. 71).

Notes

page 10: "I am not the beggar . . ." William Wilson Corcoran to Louise Morris, February 24, 1835, W. W. Corcoran Papers, Manuscript Division, Library of Congress, Washington, DC (hereafter WWC Papers).

page 10: "Your daughter is now under the protection . . ." Corcoran to Commodore Charles Morris, December 23, 1835, WWC Papers.

page 21: "Mr. Corcoran, by his magnificent entertainments . . ." Benjamin Ogle Tayloe, *Our Neighbors on La Fayette Square, Anecdotes and Reminiscences; Selections from In Memoriam* (1872; repr., Washington, DC: The League, 1982), 35.

page 29: "The [early] date of its construction . . ." Nomination for the Renwick Gallery, National Register of Historic Places, National Park Service, US Department of the Interior, Washington, DC, 1971.

page 33: "The South should have her rights . . ." Corcoran to Mr. Semmes in Memphis, Tennessee, April 24, 1861, WWC Papers, quoted in Holly Tank, "Dedicated to Art: William Corcoran and the Founding of His Gallery," *Washington History* 17 (Fall/Winter 2005): 36.

page 35: "willing that the Gvt should occupy the building . . ." Anthony Hyde to Montgomery Meigs, August 20, 1861, Records of the Quartermaster General, National Archives and Records Administration, Washington, DC, quoted in *Historic Structure Report: Smithsonian American Art Museum's Renwick Gallery, Dedicated to Art,* prepared for the Office of Facilities Engineering and Operations, Smithsonian Institution; Architrave PC, Architects (Washington, DC: 2009), IC-6.

page 35: "in the present state of the country . . ." Corcoran to James Renwick, April 10, 1861, microfilm copy in Corcoran Gallery of Art Records, Archives of American Art, Smithsonian Institution, Washington, DC (hereafter AAA).

page 39: "high tempered, unyielding . . ." Montgomery C. Meigs Papers, Manuscript Division, Library of Congress, Washington, DC (hereafter MCM Papers), quoted in David W. Miller, *Second Only to Grant: Quartermaster General Montgomery C. Meigs* (Shippensburg, PA: White Mane Books, 2000), 5.

page 40: "pulled down the active, the enterprising . . ." MCM Papers, quoted in ibid., 8.

page 42: "I do not know one . . ." Abraham Lincoln, quoted in ibid., 94.

page 48: "I venture to hope . . ." Corcoran to the trustees of the gallery, May 10, 1869, quoted in the *National Intelligencer,* Washington, DC, May 19, 1869.

page 48: "perpetual establishment and maintenance . . ." Deed and Charter of the Corcoran Gallery of Art, May 10, 1869, Corcoran Gallery of Art Archives, quoted in Sarah Cash, ed., *Corcoran Gallery of Art: American Paintings to 1945* (Washington, DC: Corcoran Gallery of Art, 2011), 24.

page 48: "in fact a national event. . . . The magnitude of this princely endowment . . ." *Washington Daily Chronicle,* May 19, 1869, quoted in William Wilson Corcoran, *A Grandfather's Legacy* (Washington, DC, 1879), 535.

page 51: "Mr. Renwick has been compelled by business . . ." A. B. Mullett and Edward Clark to J. C. Kennedy, Chairman of the Trustees' Building Committee, November 11, 1869, microfilm copy in Corcoran Gallery of Art Records, AAA.

page 56: "were carefully shielded . . ." Tank, "Dedicated to Art," 45; see also 51n66.

page 56: "a benefaction to the whole country . . ." "Art in Washington," *New York Times,* January 20, 1874, quoted in Cash, *Corcoran Gallery of Art,* 28.

page 56: "Washington may now pride herself . . ." E. A. Wiswall, "The Corcoran Gallery of Art," *The Aldine,* no. 6 (June 1874): 120, Renwick Gallery Records, Smithsonian American Art Museum, Washington, DC (hereafter Renwick Gallery Records).

page 56: "an important means of improving the intellectual . . ." *Smithsonian Institution Annual Report,* 1874, quoted in Tank, "Dedicated to Art," 39.

page 57: "make a highly creditable Louvre." "Have We a Louvre among Us?," *Philadelphia Bulletin,* May 17, 1869, quoted in Cash, *Corcoran Gallery of Art,* 27.

page 57: "Senator Sumner, who takes a natural pride . . ." *Washington Daily Chronicle,* May 19, 1869, quoted in Corcoran, *A Grandfather's Legacy,* 536.

page 58: "Some of the pictures are of a quality . . ." S. G. W. Benjamin, "The Corcoran Gallery of Art," *Century Illustrated Magazine,* no. 6 (October 1882): 825.

page 62: "The general expression amounting to . . ." Corcoran to Moses Ezekiel, June 25, 1883, WWC Papers.

page 65: "scrupulously neat in his person . . ." *Washington Evening Star,* February 25, 1888.

page 66: The millionaires of the United States in 1884 shown in fig. 45: Samuel Tilden, Leland Stanford, D. Ogden Mills, Jay Gould, John W. MacKay, Russell Sage, William Waldorf Astor, Cornelius Vanderbilt, August Belmont, James Flood, George Seney, William Wilson Corcoran, Sidney Dillon, Cyrus Field, and an unidentified gentleman.

page 82: "It may look like a Victorian horror . . ." Jacqueline Kennedy to Bernard L. Boutin, March 6, 1962, Bernard L. Boutin Personal Papers, 1955–1966, John F. Kennedy Presidential Library and Museum, Boston, copy in Renwick Gallery Records.

page 82: "the old buildings . . . are a symbol of the White House . . ." John Carl Warnecke, interview by Thomas S. Page, September 1992, quoted in Kurt Helfrich, "Modernism for Washington? The Kennedys and the Redesign of Lafayette Square," *Washington History* 8 (Spring/Summer 1996): 32.

page 83: "I just hope Jacqueline wakes up . . ." Commission of Fine Arts minutes, October 19, 1962, quoted in David A. Doheny, *David Finley: Quiet Force for America's Arts* (Washington, DC: National Trust for Historic Preservation, 2006), 317–18.

page 85: "I am enthusiastic about your suggestions . . ." Lyndon Johnson to S. Dillon Ripley, June 23, 1965, Smithsonian Institution Archives, Washington, DC, quoted in *Historic Structure Report,* IC-73.

page 91: "getting it back to the spirit . . ." Ada Louise Huxtable, "Renwick Gallery Wins Survival Battle," *New York Times,* January 28, 1972.

page 91: "[The restoration] is a triumph . . ." Wolf Von Eckardt, "Renwick: A Triumph Over Neglect," *Washington Post,* January 22, 1972.

page 91: "The Renwick Gallery restoration is a masterpiece . . ." "Renwick Gallery Acclaimed," *Washington Post,* April 27, 1974.

Selected Bibliography

Archives

Corcoran Gallery of Art. Records, 1860–1947. Archives of American Art. Smithsonian Institution, Washington, DC.

Corcoran, W. W., Papers, 1791–1896. Manuscript Division. Library of Congress, Washington, DC.

Meigs, Montgomery C., Papers, 1799–1971. Manuscript Division. Library of Congress, Washington, DC.

Rattner, Selma. Research Papers on James Renwick, 1856–2001. Drawings & Archives Collection. Avery Architectural & Fine Arts Library, Columbia University, New York.

Renwick Gallery. Records. Smithsonian American Art Museum, Washington, DC.

Renwick, James, and James Renwick Jr., Architectural Drawings and Papers. Drawings & Archives Collection. Avery Architectural & Fine Arts Library, Columbia University, New York.

Smithsonian Institution Archives, Washington, DC.

Additional Sources

Bouligny, Mary E. P. *A Tribute to W. W. Corcoran of Washington City*. Philadelphia, 1874. Michigan Historical Reprint Series, http://mirlyn.lib.umich.edu/Record/000330653.

Cantor, Jay E. "The Public Architecture of James Renwick Jr." MA thesis, University of Delaware, 1967.

Cash, Sarah. "'Encouraging American Genius': Collecting American Art at the Corcoran Gallery of Art." In *Corcoran Gallery of Art: American Paintings to 1945*, edited by Sarah Cash, in collaboration with Emily D. Shapiro and Lisa Strong, 15–43. Washington, DC: Corcoran Gallery of Art, 2011.

Cohen, David M., and George F. Hutchinson. "Lafayette Square, Marvin Jones, and the United States Court of Claims." *Journal of the Federal Circuit Historical Society* 2 (2008): 67–78.

Cohen, Henry. *Business and Politics in America from the Age of Jackson to the Civil War; The Career Biography of W. W. Corcoran*. Westport, CT: Greenwood Publishing Corp., 1971.

"The Corcoran Gallery of Art, in Washington." *The Art Journal*, n.s., 1 (1875): 143–44.

Corcoran, William Wilson. *A Grandfather's Legacy; Containing a Sketch of His Life and Obituary Notices of Some Members of His Family, Together with Letters from His Friends*. Washington, DC, 1879.

Crespo, Rafael A. "The Decoration of the Grand Gallery, Renwick Gallery of Art." Unpublished MS, October 30, 1989. Renwick Gallery Records, Smithsonian American Art Museum, Washington, DC.

———. "The Renwick Gallery (Old Corcoran Gallery)." Unpublished MS, August 21, 1989. Smithsonian Institution Archives, Washington, DC.

Dickinson, William C., Dean A. Herrin, and Donald R. Kennon, eds. *Montgomery C. Meigs and the Building of the Nation's Capital*. Athens, OH: Published for the U.S. Capitol Historical Society by Ohio University Press, 2001.

Doheny, David A. *David Finley: Quiet Force for America's Arts.* Washington, DC: National Trust for Historic Preservation, 2006.

Galop, Kathleen P., Esq. "The Historic Preservation Legacy of Jacqueline Kennedy Onassis." *Forum Journal* 20 (Spring 2006). http://www.preservationnation.org/forum/library/#.VRLQbeGd4xI.

Goode, James M. "The Renwick Gallery of the Smithsonian Institution," a brief history compiled for the Historic American Buildings Survey, Department of the Interior. Unpublished MS, March 1, 1971. Renwick Gallery Records, Smithsonian American Art Museum, Washington, DC.

Helfrich, Kurt. "Modernism for Washington? The Kennedys and the Redesign of Lafayette Square." *Washington History* 8 (Spring/Summer 1996): 16–37.

Historic Structure Report: Smithsonian American Art Museum's Renwick Gallery, Dedicated to Art. Prepared for the Office of Facilities Engineering and Operations, Smithsonian Institution, Washington, DC; Architrave PC, Architects, January 1, 2009.

Hopkins, Griffith Morgan, Jr. *Map of the District of Columbia from Official Records and Actual Surveys.* Philadelphia, 1887.

Huxtable, Ada Louise. "Renwick Gallery Wins Survival Battle." *New York Times,* January 28, 1972.

Kohler, Sue A., and Jeffrey R. Carson. "1611 H Street, N.W.: William W. Corcoran Residence." In *Sixteenth Street Architecture,* 1:9–42. Washington, DC: Commission of Fine Arts, 1978.

MacLeod, William. *Catalogue of the Paintings, Statuary, Casts, Bronzes, &c. of the Corcoran Gallery of Art.* Washington, DC, 1874.

McKenna, Rosalie Thorne. "James Renwick, Jr. and the Second Empire Style in the United States." *Magazine of Art* 44 (March 1951): 97–101.

Miller, David W. *Second Only to Grant: Quartermaster General Montgomery C. Meigs.* Shippensburg, PA: White Mane Books, 2000.

Mitchell, Mary. "William W. Corcoran and Oak Hill Cemetery." Unpublished MS, n.d. Renwick Gallery Records, Smithsonian American Art Museum, Washington, DC.

Rattner, Selma. "James Renwick (1818–1895)." In *Macmillan Encyclopedia of Architects,* edited by Adolf K. Placzek. New York: Free Press, 1982.

"The Renwick Chapel History." *News from Oak Hill,* Fall 2013, 3–10.

Tank, Holly. "Dedicated to Art: William Corcoran and the Founding of His Gallery." *Washington History* 17 (Fall/Winter 2005): 26–51.

———. "William Wilson Corcoran: Washington Philanthropist." *Washington History* 17 (Fall/Winter 2005): 52–65.

Taragin, Davira Spiro. *Corcoran.* Washington, DC: Corcoran Gallery of Art, 1976.

Trapp, Kenneth R. "Dedicated to Art: Twenty-Five Years at the Renwick Gallery." In *Skilled Work: American Craft in the Renwick Gallery,* 13–29. Washington, DC: Smithsonian Institution Press, 1998.

"A Veteran Philanthropist." *Harper's Weekly* 32 (January 7, 1888): 5.

Wallach, Alan. *Exhibiting Contradiction: Essays on the Art Museum in the United States.* Amherst: University of Massachusetts Press, 1998.

"Washington Revisited: A Twenty-Year Retrospective Review of the Architecture of Lafayette Square," transcript of presentations on April 22, 1981. *Journal of the Federal Circuit Historical Society* 2 (2008): 79–98.

Illustration Sources and Credits

Cover: ca. 1870s; Corcoran Gallery of Art Archives/National Gallery of Art, Washington; **frontispiece, pp. 6–7, Fig. 71 (detail), and back cover:** Photos by Ron Blunt, 2009; Smithsonian American Art Museum.

Mr. Corcoran
Fig. 1, Lithograph by E. Sachse & Co., Baltimore, 1855; Library of Congress; Fig. 2, Photographic print, 1893–97; The Historical Society of Washington, DC; Fig. 3, Print of etching by L. M. Guillaume, n.d.; Corcoran Gallery of Art Archives/National Gallery of Art, Washington.

Renwick and Corcoran
Fig. 4, Lithograph by W. Friend, 1856–57; The Historical Society of Washington, DC; Fig. 5, Lithograph by Charles Burton, 1849; Library of Congress; Fig. 6, ca. 1853; Museum History Photography, Photograph Archives, Smithsonian American Art Museum; Fig. 7, Photograph by Carol M. Highsmith, 2010; The George F. Landegger Collection of District of Columbia Photographs in Carol M. Highsmith's America, Library of Congress, Prints and Photographs Division; Fig. 8, Photograph, 1900–9; The Historical Society of Washington, DC; Fig. 9, Photograph, 1913–17; The Historical Society of Washington,

DC; Fig. 10, ca. 1880; Museum History Photography, Photograph Archives, Smithsonian American Art Museum; Fig. 11, ca. 1880; Donald McClelland papers, 1857–1968, Archives of American Art, Smithsonian Institution.

Design of the New Gallery
Fig. 12, Stereograph, ca. 1926; Library of Congress; Fig. 13, Map by Robert Killian and Eleni Swengler, adapted from 1887 map in Griffith Morgan Hopkins Jr., *Map of the District of Columbia from Official Records and Actual Surveys* (Philadelphia, 1887); Fig. 14, Photocopy of print, 1859; Library of Congress; Fig. 15, Photographic print, ca. 1858; Museum History Photography, Photograph Archives, Smithsonian American Art Museum; Fig. 16, Lithograph by Ferd, Mayor & Co., ca. 1862; Library of Congress; Fig. 17, Glass-negative photograph by Harris & Ewing, ca. 1910–20; Library of Congress.

The War Begins
Fig. 18, Hand-colored lithograph, Currier & Ives, New York, publisher, ca. 1861; Library of Congress; Fig. 19, Hand-colored wood engraving, ca. 1861; Northern Virginia Civil War images collection, Collection #C0150, Special Collections and Archives, George Mason University Libraries, Fairfax, VA; Fig. 20, Color lithograph, Charles Magnus,

publisher, 1864; The Albert H. Small Washingtoniana Collection, George Washington University Museum, AS 62.

General Meigs
Fig. 21, Glass-negative photograph, April 1865; Library of Congress; Fig. 22, Albumen print carte de visite, Bell & Hall, Washington, DC, publisher, ca. 1864; Smithsonian American Art Museum, Museum purchase; Fig. 23, Albumen photographic print by Andrew J. Russell, 1861–65; Library of Congress; Fig. 24, Glass-negative photograph, 1860–65; Library of Congress; Fig. 25, East front of Arlington House, albumen print by Andrew J. Russell, June 28, 1864; Library of Congress; Fig. 26, Lithograph, A. Brett & Co., New York, printer/Jones & Clark, New York, publisher, 1865; Library of Congress.

Reclaiming the Gallery
Fig. 27, Glass-negative photograph (Detroit Publishing Co., 1900–12) of 1867 painting by Charles Loring Elliott; Library of Congress; Fig. 28, ca. 1875; Museum History Photography, Photograph Archives, Smithsonian American Art Museum.

Opening the Gallery
Fig. 29, ca. 1880; Museum History Photography, Photograph Archives, Smithsonian American Art Museum;

Fig. 30, Photographic print, ca. 1871; Library of Congress; Fig. 31, ca. 1890s; Corcoran Gallery of Art Archives/ National Gallery of Art, Washington; Fig. 32, Published in William MacLeod, *Catalogue of the Corcoran Gallery of Art* (Washington, DC, 1874), reproduced from *Historic Structure Report: Smithsonian American Art Museum's Renwick Gallery, Dedicated to Art,* OFEO, Smithsonian Institution and Architrave PC, Architects (Washington, DC: 2009), appendix C–p. 6; Fig. 33, Stereograph, ca. 1875; Smithsonian Institution Archives (image #2011-1139); Fig. 34, Stereograph, ca. 1877; Corcoran Gallery of Art Archives/ National Gallery of Art, Washington; Fig. 35, ca. 1885; Museum History Photography, Photograph Archives, Smithsonian American Art Museum; Fig. 36, Photoprint on cardboard mount, 1880; National Anthropological Archives, Smithsonian Institution (INV 02064500).

The Later Years
Fig. 37, ca. 1870s; Corcoran Gallery of Art Archives/National Gallery of Art, Washington; Figs. 38–40, Photographs by Robert Killian, 2015; Fig. 41, Corcoran Gallery of Art Archives/National Gallery of Art, Washington; Fig. 42, ca. 1889; Museum History Photography, Photograph Archives, Smithsonian American Art Museum; Fig. 43, ca. 1892; Museum History Photography, Photograph Archives, Smithsonian American Art Museum; Fig. 44, Photograph by Carol M. Highsmith, 1980; The George F. Landegger Collection of District of Columbia Photographs in Carol M. Highsmith's America, Library

of Congress, Prints and Photographs Division; Fig. 45, Franklin Square Lithographic Co. (active 1880s), lithograph with tintstone on paper, 1884; National Portrait Gallery, Smithsonian Institution (NPG.85.54); Fig. 46, ca. 1886; Museum History Photography, Photograph Archives, Smithsonian American Art Museum; Fig. 47, Photograph, ca. 1960; Donald McClelland papers, 1857–1968, Archives of American Art, Smithsonian Institution; Fig. 48, Thomas Hicks, pastel on paper, 1863; The Frick Art Reference Library, New York; Fig. 49, Photograph by Mathew Brady, Washington, DC, Sept. 1882; Library of Congress; Fig. 50, Photographic print, ca. 1890; Library of Congress.

The Court of Claims
Figs. 51, 53, ca. 1920; Museum History Photography, Photograph Archives, Smithsonian American Art Museum; Fig. 52, Photograph, ca. 1960; Donald McClelland papers, 1857–1968, Archives of American Art, Smithsonian Institution; Fig. 54, Photograph, 1924/1945; The Historical Society of Washington, DC; Fig. 55, Photograph, ca. 1958; Library of Congress; Fig. 56, undated photograph by Bayart Reid; Architect of the Capitol, Washington, DC.

Saving the Building
Fig. 57 (detail), Photograph by Abbie Rowe, 1962; White House Photographs, John F. Kennedy Presidential Library and Museum, Boston; Fig. 58, Photograph by Robert Knudsen, 1962; White House Photographs, John F. Kennedy Presidential Library and Museum, Boston.

Restoring the Building
Fig. 59, Photograph by Harry B. Neufeld, 1973; Smithsonian Institution Archives (image #73-4540-7A); Fig. 60, Photograph by Harry B. Neufeld, 1974; Smithsonian Institution Archives (image #74-945-44); Fig. 61, 1972; *New York Times*; Fig. 62, ca. 1985; Museum History Photography, Photograph Archives, Smithsonian American Art Museum; Fig. 63, ca. 1975; Museum History Photography, Photograph Archives, Smithsonian American Art Museum.

The Renwick Today
Figs. 64, 65, ca. 1975; Museum History Photography, Photograph Archives, Smithsonian American Art Museum; Fig. 66, Photograph by Dane A. Penland, 1985; Smithsonian Institution Archives (image #85-10538-15A); Fig. 67, Photograph by Joshua Yetman, May 6, 2011; Fig. 68, 1976; Museum History Photography, Photograph Archives, Smithsonian American Art Museum; Fig. 69, author photograph, Photograph by Gene Young, 2015; Smithsonian American Art Museum; Fig. 70, Photograph by Prakash Patel, 2015; Consigli Construction Co., Inc.

Index

Page numbers in *italics* indicate illustrations.

"American Louvre," 9, 57–58
Arlington Hotel, Washington, DC, *26*, 49
Arlington House and Cemetery, Washington, DC, 44, *44, 45*, 71

Barye, Antoine-Louis, 53, 54, *55*
Beaux-Arts style, 64, *65*
Blair House, Washington, DC, 85
Boutin, Bernard L., 81–82, 83

Canova, Antonio, 61, 62
Church, Frederic, 58
Civil War (1861–65), *32*, 33, *34*, 35, *36–37*, 37, *38*, 39, *40*
Clark, Edward, 51, 64
Corcoran, Louise (Mrs. George Eustis Jr.), 10, 33, 35, 37, 47
Corcoran, Louise Amory Morris (Mrs. W. W. Corcoran), 10, 47
Corcoran, William Wilson, *12, 46*, 67
  art collection, 21–22, *22*, 25, 37, *50*, 53, 55
  biographical details, 9–10, 33, 35, 37, 47, 65, 67, 68, *68*
  business career, 10, 11, *11*, 13, *13*, 15, 67
  Civil War period and aftermath, 33, 35, *36–37*, 37, 47
  European travels, 13, 25, 35, 37, 47
  houses and other buildings in Washington, DC, *26*
    Arlington Hotel, *26*, 49
    Corcoran and Riggs Bank, 11, *11*, 13, 15, *26*
    Corcoran building, *26*, 68
    Harewood, 19, 35, *36–37*
    Louise Home, 49, *49*
    mansion, Lafayette Square, *20–21*, 21, 22, *23, 26*, 35, 78
    town houses, 19, *19, 26*

philanthropy, 19, 21, 49, 67–68
portrait, *46*, 49, 55, 86
profile in bronze, 61–62, *62*
Renwick, collaborations with, 7, 9, 18, *18*, 19, *19*, 21, 25, 27, 35, 68
social circle, 11, 15, 21, 35, 47, 52–53
Washington Monument, Washington, DC, 21, 51–52, 53
wealth, *12*, 18–19, 66, 67
Corcoran and Riggs Bank, Washington, DC, 11, *11*, 13, 15, *26*
Corcoran Gallery of Art, Washington, DC, 64–65, *65*
Corcoran Gallery of Art (later Renwick Gallery), Washington, DC, 7, *26, 27*, 40, 99
  Apache Indians, visit by, 58, *59*
  Apollo Belvedere (plaster cast), *56, 57*
  art school, 64, *64*, 77, *77*
  ball for Washington's birthday (1871), 52–53
  baptistery doors (replicas of Ghiberti bronzes), 53, 56
  Barye sculptures, 53, 54, *55*
  bronze lions (copies of Canova sculptures), 62, *63*, 73
  catalogue, *54*, 56, *63*
  Civil War period and aftermath, 33, *34*, 35, *35*, 39, *40*, 47, 51
  Corcoran's initials, 62, *62*
  Corcoran's portrait, *46*, 49, 55, 86
  Corcoran's profile in bronze, 61–62, *62*
  corncob capitals, 29, 62, *62*
  Court of Claims period. *See* Court of Claims
  "Dedicated to Art" inscription, 2, 9, 29, *98*, 99
  demolition plans, 78, 81–83
  design and building, 25, 27–30, 51, *54*
  exterior and exterior decoration, 28–29, 35, 47, *60*, 61, 62, *62*, 77, 86

facades, 9, *27*, 29, *60, 61, 62*, 73, *74*, 77, 78
as the first art museum in America, 7, 9, 29, 48, 99
grand stairway, 29
The Greek Slave (Powers), 22, 29, 54, *56*
Hall of Bronzes, 54, *54, 55*
interior and interior decoration, 29, 35, 62–64, *63*, 87
and the Louvre, Paris, 7, 9, *24*, 25, 27, 57–58
main picture gallery (Grand Salon), *28*, 29, 39, *50*, 53, *54*, 54–55, 62–63, *63*, 72, 74, 75, 87–89
metal cresting, *2, 6, 28*, 77, *79*, 86
Octagon Room, *28*, 29, 54, *54, 56*, 87, 89
opening (1874), 54, 55–58
Parthenon frieze (plaster cast), 53, 55, *57*
praise and criticism, 56–58
relocation, 64–65, *65*
renaming, 7, 86
restoration (1967–72), 85–86, 91–92
Sculpture Hall, *54*, 55–56, *57*
sculptures on facade (Ezekiel), *60*, 61–62, *62*, 73, *74*, 86, *86*
trustees, 47–48, 51, 53, 58, 61, 63, 64, 73
Corcoran mansion, Lafayette Square, Washington, DC, *20–21*, 21, *22, 23, 26*, 35, 78
Court of Claims, Washington, DC, 73, 74, *76*, 77, 78, 83
  in Corcoran Gallery building, 7, 72, 73, 74, *75*, 78, *79*, 83, 86
  courtroom, *72*, 74
  docket room, 74, *75*
  parking garage, 77, *77*
Crawford, Thomas, 61

Davis, Jefferson, 33, 41, 47

Eustis, George, Jr., 33, 35, 37
Ezekiel, Moses, 61–62, *62*, 73, *74, 74*

Falconer, William H., 51
Fay, Paul, 82
Finley, David E., 78, 79, *80*, 81
Flagg, Ernest, 64
Fort Sumter, SC, *32*, 33
Freedom (Crawford), 61

Georgetown, DC, *8–9*, 9, 19
Ghiberti, Lorenzo, 53, 56
Grace Episcopal Church, New York, *16*, 17
Grant, Ulysses, 52, *52*, 55
The Greek Slave (Powers), 22, 29, 54, *56*

Harewood, Washington, DC, 19, 35, *36–37*
Henry, Joseph, 15, 25, 47
Herman, Lloyd E., *87*, 91, 95
Hyde, Anthony, 47, 67–68

Jacobsen, Hugh Newell, 86–87, 91
Johnson, Lyndon B., 78, 85
Jones, Marvin, 78

Kennedy, Jacqueline Bouvier (Mrs. John F.), *80*, 81–82, 83, *83*
Kennedy, John F., 79, *80*, 82, 83

Lafayette Square, Washington, DC,
   Corcoran mansion, *20–21*, 21, 22, 23, *26*, 35, 78
   redevelopment, 78, 81–83, *83*
Lee, Mary Randolph Custis (Mrs. Robert E.), 44
Lee, Robert E., 41, 44, *45*, 49
Leonardo da Vinci (Ezekiel), 61, *74*
Lincoln, Abraham, 33, 42, 45, *45*, 47
Louise Home, Washington, DC, 49, *49*
Louvre, Paris, 7, 9, *24*, 25, 27, 57
Lowe, Harry, *87*
Lucchetti, Renato, 86

MacLeod, William, *52*, 53, 56, 58
Meigs, Charles D., 39
Meigs, Mary Montgomery (Mrs. Charles D.), 39
Meigs, Montgomery Cunningham, 39–41, *41*, *42*, *42*, 43–45, *45*, 47, 70, *70–71*, *71*
Metropolitan Museum of Art, New York, 58, 70
Mullett, Alfred B., 31, 51
Murillo (replica of Ezekiel sculpture), 61, 86, *86*

Napoleon III wing, Louvre, Paris, 7, *24*, 25, 27

Niagara (Church), 58; see 59
Norfolk Botanical Gardens, VA, 73, *74*, 86, *86*

Oak Hill Cemetery, Georgetown, DC, *18*, 19, 47, 68, *68*

Paley, Albert, 95, *95*
Pennsylvania Avenue, Washington, DC, 11, 25, 29, *31*, 76
Pension Building (later National Building Museum), Washington, DC, 70–71, *71*
Powers, Hiram, 22, *56*

Quartermaster Corps, Union army, *34*, 35, *38*, 39, 42–43, 45, 47, 48, 51

Reed, Nathaniel, *84*
Renwick, James, Jr., *17*, 69
   architectural practice, 15, *16*, 17, *17*, 68–69, *69*
   architectural projects
      Charity Hospital, Blackwell's Island, New York, 30
      Corcoran building, Washington, DC, *26*, 68
      Corcoran mansion, Lafayette Square, Washington, DC, *20–21*, 21, *26*
      Grace Episcopal Church, New York, *16*, 17
      Harewood, Washington, DC, 19
      Oak Hill Cemetery chapel, Georgetown, DC, *18*, 19
      Smithsonian "Castle," Washington, DC, *14*, 15, 18–19
      St. Patrick's Cathedral, New York, 17, *17*
      town houses, Washington, DC, 19, *19*, 26
      Vassar College, Poughkeepsie, NY, 30, *30*
   biographical details, 15, 17, 25, 68, 69–70
   Corcoran, collaborations with, 7, 9, 18, *18*, 19, *19*, 21, 25, 27, 35, 68
Renwick, James, Sr., 15
Renwick, Margaret Brevoort (Mrs. James, Sr.), 15
Renwick Alliance, 95
Renwick Gallery, Washington DC (formerly Corcoran Gallery of Art), *2*, *6–7*, *94*
   American craft and decorative arts collections, 7, 85, 91, 93, 95–96
   "Dedicated to Art" inscription, *2*, *98*, 99

facades, 86, *86*, *92*, 92–93, *93*, *94*
gates (Paley), 95, *95*
Grand Salon, 86–87, *87*, 88–89
grand stairway, *90*
interior and interior decoration, 87, *87*, 88–89
metal cresting, 86
as a National Historic Landmark, *84*, 92
Octagon Room, 87, *89*
opening, 7, 91, 93
renovation (2013–15), 96, *96*, *97*
restoration (1967–72), 85–86, 91–92
sculptures on facade, 86, *86*
Riggs, George Washington, 11, 47
Ripley, S. Dillon, *84*, 85, 86

Second Empire style, 29–31, *30*, 31
Smithson, James, 15
Smithsonian Institution, 15, 56–57, 58, 70, 85, 92, 95, 99
   "Castle," *14*, 15, 18–19
St. Patrick's Cathedral, New York, 17, *17*
Stanton, Edwin M., 44, 47
State, War, and Navy Building (later Eisenhower Executive Office Building), Washington, DC, 25, 31, *31*, 76, 78
Stiepevich, Vincent G., *63*, 63–64, 86

Tayloe, Benjamin Ogle, 21

US Capitol building, Washington, DC, 29, 41–42, 51, 61

Victorian art and architecture, 64, 78, 82, 87, *87*, 88–89
Visconti, Louis, 25

Walter, Thomas U., 19, 41–42
Walters, William T., 47, 53
Warnecke, John Carl, 82–83, *83*, 86, 91
Washington, George, *23*, 52
Washington Aqueduct Bridge (later Cabin John Bridge), 41, *41*
Washington Monument, Washington, DC, 21, 51–52, 53, 58
Westlake Reed Leskosky, 96

American Louvre:
A History of the Renwick Gallery Building

Published on the occasion of the reopening of the
Renwick Gallery, November 2015

Chief, Publications: Theresa J. Slowik
Designer: Robert Killian
Editor: Mary J. Cleary
Permissions coordinator: Amy Doyel

 Smithsonian American Art Museum

The Smithsonian American Art Museum is home to one of the
largest collections of American art in the world. Its holdings—
more than 42,000 works—tell the story of America through
the visual arts and represent the most inclusive collection of
American art of any museum today. It is the nation's first federal
art collection, predating the 1846 founding of the Smithsonian
Institution. The Museum celebrates the exceptional creativity
of the nation's artists, whose insights into history, society, and
the individual reveal the essence of the American experience.

The Renwick Gallery became the home of the Museum's
American craft and decorative arts program in 1972. The
Gallery is located in a historic architectural landmark on
Pennsylvania Avenue at 17th Street, Washington, DC.

For information on other publications, write: Office
of Publications, Smithsonian American Art Museum,
MRC 970, PO Box 37012, Washington, DC 20013-7012.

Visit the Museum's website at AmericanArt.si.edu.

©2015 Smithsonian American Art Museum
All rights reserved. No part of this book may be reproduced
or used in any forms or by any means—graphic, electronic,
or mechanical, including photocopying, recording, taping, or
information storage and retrieval systems—without written
permission of the Smithsonian American Art Museum.

Printed in Italy

Library of Congress Cataloging-in-Publication Data

Smithsonian American Art Museum.
  American Louvre : a history of the Renwick Gallery building /
Charles J. Robertson.
      pages cm
  Includes bibliographical references and index.
  ISBN 978-1-907804-81-6 (softcover)
  1. Renwick Gallery—History. 2. Corcoran, W. W. (William
Wilson), 1798-1888. 3. Renwick, James, 1818-1895. 4. Art museum
architecture—Washington (D.C.) 5. Washington (D.C.)—
Buildings, structures, etc. I. Robertson, Charles (Charles J.),
author. II. Broun, Elizabeth, writer of foreword. III. Title.
  N857.A825 2015
  727'.709753—dc23

                                      2015014967

ISBN 978-1-907804-81-6 (softcover)

Cover: Corcoran Gallery of Art building (now the Renwick
Gallery), ca. 1870s

Title page: Center pavilion; back cover: Lion head. Photos by
Ron Blunt, 2009